the holy land
today
Ancient Sites
Beirut
(Beyrouth)
LEBANON
Saida
(Sidon)
Damascus
Sarafand
(Zarephath)
Qatana
Kiswe
Merj Uyun
Sur
(Tyre)
Shemona
Dan
Kedesh
Hulata
S Y R I A
Acre
Safad
GALILEE
Capernaum
Tabigha
Sea of Galilee
Mediterranean
Haifa
Tiberias
Fig
Nazareth
MT. TABOR
MT. CARMEL
Afiqim
JEBEL ED DRUZ
Dor
Afula
Der'a
River
Megiddo
Beit Shean
(Beth-shan)
Caesarea
Taanach
Ajlun
Jarash
(Gerasa)
Sea
Sebastiya
(Samaria)
Nablus
Jordan
MT. GERIZIM
Shechem
Er Rummon
Tel Aviv-Jaffa
Petah Tiqva
Ramat Gan
Es Salt
Safut
Shiloh
Lydda (Lod)
Amman
(Rabath-ammon)
Rehovot
Modin
Jericho
Jericho
Hisban
(Heshbon)
Gezer
Ramallah
Jerusalem
Ashdod
Eizariya
(Bethany)
MT. NEBO
Jiza
Beit
Shemesh
Bethlehem
Ascalon
Beth-zur
Lachish
Dead Sea
Gaza
Hebron
Ein Gedi
GAZA
STRIP
Ziklag
Gerar
Masada
Beersheba
Arad
ISRAEL
Sedom
Safi
Aina
Sede Boqer
Tafila
Shirta
Kadesh-barnea
NEGEV
Wadi 'Araba
Petra
EGYPT
SINAI
PENINSULA
J O R D A N
Ein Netafim
Ezion-geber (Elath)
Eilat (Elath)
Aqaba

A GIFT FROM
JOHN "L." WEBB

Buried Treasure in Bible Lands

BURIED TREASURE IN BIBLE LANDS

BY LENORE COHEN

THE WARD RITCHIE PRESS

By the same author

BIBLE TALES FOR VERY YOUNG CHILDREN, BOOKS 1 AND 2

CAME LIBERTY BEYOND OUR HOPE: A STORY OF HANUKKAH

Library of Congress Catalog Card Number 65-24169
Lithographed in the United States by Anderson, Ritchie & Simon
Designed by Joseph Simon

For
Rabbi Alfred Gottschalk
in gratitude
and
Stanton Macdonald Wright
artist, teacher, friend
who first introduced me to the
civilizations of the East

ACKNOWLEDGMENTS

FIRST OF ALL, I want to thank Hebrew Union College-Jewish Institute of Religion at Los Angeles for its aid, encouragement and the use of its library. I am indebted to Dr. Nelson Glueck and Dr. Paul Steinberg for the opportunity to attend the Summer Institute of Hebrew Union College Biblical and Archaeological School in Jerusalem. To Dr. Frank Moore Cross, Jr., for his kind interest; to Dr. Michael Meyer, Dr. Jack P. Lewis, Brother Dominic Ruegg, F.S.C., Dr. S. Dean McBride, Jr., and Dr. Robert Arris of the Los Angeles County Museum of History and Science, who took the time to read my manuscript and gave me many valuable suggestions; to my readers Ruth Cohen, Myrtle Spitz, Nell Mendelson, Jeannie Gottschalk, Bedene Greenspan, I give my sincere thanks, as well to Jeanne Kaufman, librarian at Hebrew Union College, Los Angeles, and Joyce and Barry Berkov.

Camel Market at Beersheba.

INTRODUCTION

THE BURIED TREASURES in Bible Lands are not all archaeological. Biblical archaeology has brought to light the literature, art, law, technology, history, customs and religious ideas of the ancient world. This book is a survey of that world from prehistory to Roman times from the findings of Biblical archaeologists and anthropologists.

A chapter is devoted to the men and women who made the archaeological discoveries, with but a cursory glance at the nineteenth-century environment of these pioneers. Briefly we note contemporary ideologies that were reinterpreted from cultural anthropological theories resulting from the discovery of the Stone Age, and prehistoric man. This is pertinent to our story because in the 1920's prehistoric man was found to have lived in Palestine.

The Bible is a product of the ancient world. Until very recently our knowledge of that world was very scant. People at the beginning of the nineteenth century had no idea of what an Assyrian or an Assyrian palace really looked like. They had read about Assyrians in the Bible, particularly (II Kings 18:13): "Now in the fourteenth year of king Hezekiah did Sennacherib king of Assyria come up against all the fenced cities of Judah and took them. And Hezekiah king of Judah sent to the king of Assyria to Lachish, saying, 'I have offended; return from me; that which thou puttest on me will I bear.'" It goes on to tell how Hezekiah paid to Sennacherib three hundred talents of silver and the treasures of the king's house as a bribe not to destroy Jerusalem.

By the middle of the nineteenth century, people could visit the British Museum in London and actually see a sculptured portrait of Sennacherib sitting on his throne outside the walls of the besieged city of Lachish, inspecting booty and a procession of Israelites who had been taken prisoner. These bas reliefs also showed how the Israelites dressed and how they defended their city walls. All this was possible because a British archaeologist, Austen Henry Layard, had dug up Sennacherib's palace at Nineveh in the early nineteenth century.

About eighty-three years later, in 1932, another British archaeologist, James Leslie Starkey, made it possible for the twentieth-century Bible readers to locate the city of Lachish in Israel. He dug the city out of a mound south of Jerusalem. The defenses of Lachish were built exactly as the Assyrian artists had carved them in stone in the seventh century B.C.

Until the beginning of the nineteenth century, the ancient world of Assyria, Babylonia, and Egypt slept in ruined peace under the soil of centuries. Through archaeology their existence became a fact, their contributions to our contemporary civilization staggeringly great.

Scientific archaeological excavation did not really begin in Palestine until after World War I and the British Mandate. The British and American Schools in old Jerusalem which is now situated in Jordan made many important discoveries which will be discussed in the succeeding pages. The French excavations in Syria were among the most exciting discoveries of this period. The Hebrew University, at that time located on Mount Scopus, made great archaeological contributions.

All work stopped during World War II. Then in 1947 the Dead Sea Scrolls were discovered and threw new light on Biblical studies. The British and American Schools in Jordan continue their excavations. French, Italian, and other scholars from all over the world carry on archaeological studies. The State of Israel through its Department of Antiquities has a full-time program of archaeological exploration.

In subsequent chapters many of these discoveries will be discussed. First, it might be a good idea to take a quick trip around modern Israel to understand the climate and geography. Then it will be helpful to visit an excavation and even dig a bit. It may be necessary to familiarize ourselves with archaeological periods, pottery styles, and a few techniques. All this makes archaeology come alive, and helps the Bible take its place in history.

CONTENTS

LIST OF ILLUSTRATIONS

PAGE

Buried Treasure in Bible Lands

CHAPTER I

PALESTINE IS THE HOLY LAND

PALESTINE IS THE Holy Land to Jew, Christian and Moslem. The name is not found in the Bible. It was coined by the Greeks who called the Philistine-inhabited coastal plain Philistia. Herodotus and other Latin authors described all of ancient Israel as Palestine, and since Roman times the name of the area has been Palestine. Today Palestine has been divided into the states of Israel, Jordan, Lebanon, and Syria. Touching its southern borders are Saudi-Arabia and Egypt.

In this book we consider the influences on the Bible of all the ancient peoples linked together by the crescent-shaped Mediterranean coast of western Asia, and called the Fertile Crescent. If the Fertile Crescent were lighted up by a crescent-shaped new moon the illuminated territories would be the Tigris and Euphrates Valleys in the east, the Nile Valley in the south, Palestine and Syria in the west, with the northern horn of the crescent touching the eastern tip of Asia Minor. In the shadows of the crescent would be Persia to the east, Cyprus and the Aegean islands west in the Mediterranean, and the bulk of Asia Minor sprawling northwest into Europe.

Our archaeological story is essentially that of Palestine. Is it really the Holy Land?—A land of milk and honey as reported by

Benedictine monk, Bernard of Cluny, who wrote of Jerusalem:

"Jerusalem the golden
With milk and honey blest,
Beneath thy contemplation
Sink heart and voice oppressed:
I know not, oh I know not,
What social joys are there;
What radiancy of glory,
What light beyond compare!"

Palestine is of this earth. It is a land of rugged mountains, barren hills, rocky caves, fertile valleys and golden deserts. Situated on the eastern end of the Mediterranean it is close to Africa and Europe. Modern Israel by jet plane is only twelve and one-half hours from New York.

Let us be passengers on that jet plane that has just landed at Lod Airport in Israel. We whiz through customs and seat ourselves in a Tel Aviv-bound sight-seeing bus, and immediately look out the window for a Biblical scene depicted in the cinema or in paintings found in museums. The scene is a snarl of plywood and plaster white stucco houses, shops and filling stations with neon signs, honking motor cars, and people dressed as we are.

As the bus rolls forward the guide tells us over the microphone that in the second century A.D. Lod was called Jamnia and was a seat of Jewish learning. Now if we will crane our necks and look down a side street as the bus slows we will see St. George Church. We stare at a nineteenth-century church in need of a coat of paint as the guide informs us that St. George was born here in the fourth century A.D.

Soon we are riding through a wide plain of cultivated fields, and learn from the guide that this is the plain of Ono mentioned in the Holy Scriptures (Nehemiah 6:2). Now we are able to look in all directions as the bus takes its turns to approach the beach hotel where we will stay. Back of us brown treeless mountains of the Western Range ring the sky. Ahead of us is a straight line of white surf as blue waves lap the beaches.

We find Tel Aviv a modern city charged with vitality and action. It is a kaleidoscope of imposing aluminum and glass public buildings, prison-like apartment houses with endless tiers of balconies, sidewalk cafés, flowering eucalyptus trees, a cosmopolitan population from all corners of the diaspora: golden-skinned Orientals, swarthy north Africans, blond Europeans, pale, in-bred orthodox Polish Jews who still wear the flat black hats, long overcoats and side curls like their ancestors who settled here in the nineteenth century.

We leave Tel Aviv and begin our tour of Israel by travelling north to Haifa. We watch the rolling panorama of the coastal plain rich with citrus groves, fields of grapes, banana plantations, vegetable gardens, and at last the bustling port of picturesque Haifa where the mountains meet the sea. Thus far our trip is as familiar as traveling in the United States.

After the bus leaves Haifa and climbs up a sinuous road to the top of Mount Carmel the familiar panorama disappears. We look down on the valley of Jezreel almost folded away in mountains. The geometrically-shaped fields look like an abstract painting. We feel isolated from the cities of the coastal plain.

Our guide tells us that this feeling of isolation is characteristic of the geography of Israel, for the country is divided into four belts running north and south: (1) the Coastal Plain; (2) the Central Range which stretches from Lebanon through Galilee to the tableland of the Negev; (3) the Jordan Valley which reaches through its various sections to the Red Sea; and (4) the Eastern Range which slopes away on the east to Transjordan.

We have left the Coastal Plain and are now viewing from the north the southern end of Galilee where it is cut by the Valley of Jezreel or Esdraelon, as it is sometimes called.

To the south are the hills of Samaria which form the geographical center of the country, and in the heart of that district is Mount Gerizim. The Samaritan religious group had its center on Mount Gerizim. Another section of the Hill Country is Judah, where Jerusalem is located. The lowlands or Shephelah of Judah are on the western side of this watershed of hills and clouds from the Mediterranean bring in rainfall so that farming is possible. The eastern side is called the "Wilderness of Judah" and leads to the Dead Sea. The hills gradually descend to the tableland of the Negev and the city of Beersheba and in the south to Kadesh-barnea.

Our next viewing point is Mount Tabor, where we look down on the Jordan Valley which is the third north and south belt. The floor of the Jordan Valley is deep green, and dotted with vague blue patches which our guide tells us are fish ponds and the Sea of Galilee which is also called Lake Tiberius or Lake Gennesaret. When the first Jewish settlement was founded in Upper Galilee in 1892 this valley was marshland, full of malaria, and the nights echoed with the yapping and wailing of jackals and hyenas. The source of the Jordan is at the foot of snow-covered Mt. Hermon, which was the frontier of Og, King of Bashan (Joshua 13:12). The Jordan river flows south to Lake Huleh which is 6 feet above sea level. Modern Israel has straightened the Jordan bed as it exists from Lake Huleh, drained the swamps and opened that section of the valley to cultivation. When the river enters the Sea of Galilee it has dropped to 690 feet below sea level. After the Jordan leaves the Sea of Galilee it flows 220 miles south to the Dead Sea which is 1,300 feet below sea level. On the way to the Dead Sea the river snakes through a valley only 2½ miles wide at some points. Jericho is situated at the widest point of this southern section of the river valley which is 12 miles across.

Now as the bus goes down, down, down from Mount Tabor to the city of Tiberius we learn that this land is below sea level because of a depression called the Jordan Rift, which extends from Syria through the Red Sea into the heart of East Africa. The Jordan Rift in Israel divides the country into the upper Jordan valley to the Sea of Galilee; the middle section of the rift extends from the Sea of Galilee to the Dead Sea; the third section is the Arabah valley which stretches 100 miles from the Dead Sea to the Red Sea or Gulf of Eilat.

To the east of the Jordan valley is the fourth belt or Plateau of Transjordan. East of the Dead Sea were the Biblical lands of Moab and Edom. Here were located picturesque Petra which we will discuss later and the main highway across the desert to Mesopotamia from Gaza, Egypt, and Phoenicia.

What a variety of landscapes! Wherever you go you have the feeling or illusion of self-containment. Now we are beginning to understand why there were 33 kings in Canaan when Joshua entered the country, and why the country was only under one rule during the times of King Solomon and Alexander Jannai the

Maccabean king. No wonder it was difficult to bring this country under a single rule in ancient times when there were no roads, and the mountains were riddled with caves where rebels could hide.

South from Galilee to Jerusalem the remains of ancient rock terraces form balconies on the barren mountains, and from the heights we see vistas of the wilderness only five miles distant. Modern Jerusalem is a quiet, academic city, the rock-faced new buildings blending with the landscape. Our journey heads us south through reforested mountains, where every tree has been a gift, to Beersheba, capitol of the Negev. The sun shines harshly on this busy city with the real flavor of the Orient, from the dark-robed Bedouins to the French-speaking Moroccans. Palm fronds glitter like silver in front of our modern hotel, and the desert is oatmeal-colored as it stretches away to the brown and ochre mountains which clouds shadow with spots of purple.

Here is the climate boundary of Israel. A straight line running from Gaza to the Dead Sea divides the rain-receiving north from the arid Negev. Ninety per cent of the population lives in the north. Now that the State of Israel has piped water to the Negev, irrigated fields of cotton turn the desert green around Beersheba. Methods of dry farming and water conservation are opening new areas for cultivation, and our guide tells us that 1,900 years ago a people called the Nabataeans farmed this area very successfully through water conservation. Later on in this book we will find out more about the Nabataeans.

Now our bus takes us south through the empty triangular Negev covering about 4,000 square miles to its point at Eilat, the Red Sea port of Israel. On the way we pass Solomon's copper mines, pick up souvenirs of slag atop an ancient hill where copper was smelted, and pass the modern smelter. At Eilat we swim in a warm sea whose waters are jade green and turquoise matrix, like the jewelry we buy at Eilat. We wonder why the sea is called Red.

We skirt Beersheba on our return to the north, to ride past jagged, knife-backed mountains with precipitous cliffs to the sky-blue Dead Sea. There a thriving chemical industry produces potash and bromine. We stop at a recreation area where Israel has provided fresh water showers, so that we can float like corks on this sea of salt, and yet wash ourselves clean. This fresh water comes from the exquisite oasis of Ein Gedi, green with trees and green pasture. We see a stream of silver falling from the height of a mountain; this is the ancient waterfall called David's Fountain. The water drops over the rocks into two pools, one above the other, and we swim in both of them showering in the cool, delicious waterfalls.

There is a haunting eternity about those mountains and deserts, a soothing greenness in the valleys, and peace by the ocean, or on the shores of the Sea of Galilee and the River Jordan. We begin to understand why men long ago found inspiration in this land and produced the Bible . . . and now we know and feel that this is the Holy Land.

CHAPTER II

LET'S GO ON A DIG!

LET'S GO ON a dig at Tell Arad in southern Israel where a modern archaeological excavation is in progress. At Arad, an ancient Canaanite fortress in the northern Negev, the first Israelite invasion was checked. We learn this from the Bible (Numbers 21:1): "When the Canaanite, the king of Arad, who dwelt in the Negeb, heard that Israel was coming by the way of Atharim, he fought against Israel and took some of them captive." This defeat caused Moses to change his tactics, and decide to enter Canaan from the east by way of Jericho. The people began to grumble (Numbers 21:5): "Wherefore have ye brought us up out of Egypt to die in the wilderness?"

Moses made a realistic decision because Arad was well fortified and controlled the north and south roads between Palestine and Egypt. Before Tell Arad was excavated the only authority for the military strength of Arad was the Bible. The evidence that this ancient fortress did exist was one of the rewards of going on a dig.

Before excavation, Tell Arad was tall enough to be mistaken for a mountain. High she stood among the surrounding hills, like a huge woman securely wrapped in a great bulging cloak—a cloak made of sand, rock and soil. Inside the cloak were the remains of 5,000 years of human occupancy. These remains were scraps of things that men had built, like foundations of buildings, stone tools, pieces of pottery called sherds, figurines, copper ornaments, bronze weapons, objects of iron and glass.

Archaeologists Yohanan Aharoni and Ruth Amiran found the

Courtesy Israel Exploration Society

General view of Tell Arad from Early Bronze city showing wall and one of the semi-circular towers.

head of this proud old mound close to the surface when they began to excavate in the spring of 1962. The mound had a Roman fortress for a head. This had been converted into a khan or inn for travelers during the Arab period. The excavators discovered a hidden treasure of glassware and other objects in one of the rooms. This treasure may have been concealed when the place was abandoned.

The cloak of the mound was so securely fastened to her neck that the archaeologists opened it bit by bit.

First, they dug a trench in a straight line from the top of the mound to its foot. The purpose of the trench was to find out where buildings were located, and the different levels of occupation. Pottery sherds found between the walls established the dates of the various levels. The mound of Tell Arad consisted of a small, high citadel and a large lower city. Two seasons of work revealed seventeen levels of strata of habitation, beginning with the Chalcolithic period (ca. 3500 B.C.) and ending in the Arab period (ca. A.D. 800). Excavation began with the high mound, uncovering various fortresses from the time of Solomon to the Romans. The lower city began with a Chalcolithic village which was unfortified. This was deserted before the beginning of the third millennium B.C. An Early Bronze Age city was built (ca. 3000 B.C.) and covered an area of about 25 acres.

Now we are beginning to understand why Tell Arad like all Tells is a man-made mountain. How did it grow so high? If the first village was built 5,000 years ago at the level of the plain, the others must have been built on top of it. Let us suppose the first town was destroyed by enemies and the people deserted it. The enemies took over the town, leveled the ruins, and built a new town on top of the debris. Consequently the second town was higher than the first. The people who had been forced to flee left behind many of their possessions including much broken pottery. This was swept into the debris. Pottery sherds which are indestructible have survived all these centuries and millenniums at Tell Arad. Regarding this indestructibility, Nelson Glueck wrote in his book, *Rivers in the Desert*: "Pottery can be shattered, but the pieces will remain, indeed have remained intact for thousands of years." Visualize thousands of years where towns were leveled, others built on the ruins, and you can see the mound rising. Sometimes towns lasted for centuries and slowed the rise of the mound. Why did people keep building towns in one particular spot? Tell Arad must have had a good water supply. A source of water is very important in Palestine where rainfall is scanty.

Excavations in Palestine usually take place in the late spring or summer after the rainy season. When we arrived at Tell Arad in July of 1964, the excavation had been in progress for two seasons.

An excavation in the Negev in July is a hot place. The soil is dry and dusty, and a lazy wind may or may not blow in from the ocean. Nights are cool and so are the early mornings. The hour of five in the morning is rising time for excavation workers. By six o'clock we volunteers are seated on side benches in back of a truck, appropriately straw-hatted, canvas-gloved, wearing jeans or shorts, and are anxious to start excavating.

The truck rolls down the pavement in the cool, clear morning. Suddenly there is a lurch! A cloud of dust obscures our vision, and as it clears we see we are bumping along a narrow dirt road fringed with golden stubbles from recently harvested grain fields.

An abrupt stop throws us against each other. The driver suggests we stretch our legs, because a large flock of black goats and shaggy fat-tailed sheep have fanned out across the road. We watch a black-robed Bedouin shepherdess and her small daughter clear the highway of animals. Her black robes flying in the breeze, the Bedouin woman, shouting Arabic commands, expertly drives the herd forward by prodding them with a stick. She faces us with a friendly smile, and we are fascinated by the ring in her nose, and the green tattooed designs on her face. She knows the driver. Her husband and son are working at the excavation. Now that the crop of winter grain has been harvested, they are glad to work for a pound and a half a day, about 50 cents in our money.

During this interlude we have discovered that one of the volunteers worked on the excavation last season. Riding again in the truck we ply him with questions, and he willingly becomes our guide. "That's the citadel of Tell Arad straight ahead," he tells us.

As we pass a low hill some Arab workmen are getting out of a truck, and our guide says, "This is the lower city of Arad, which dates back to the early Canaanite period or Early Bronze Ages, one and two."

"That should be about 3100 to 2700 B.C.," says one of our group named Bill, who always has his nose in a guide book.

The guide nods and points in a circle. "Imagine this whole area surrounded by a stone wall over two meters thick. See that ridge of hills?"

We all stare at a semicircle of small hills.

"The line of that stone wall was traced along the ridge for more than a kilometer." As we follow the guide's moving arm, he tells us that three projecting semicircular towers were discovered on the wall. This discovery has been very exciting to the archaeologists, for Arad presents for the first time the general plan and fortification of an Early Bronze city in Palestine.

Quoting the guide book, Bill reminds him that similar fortresses have been excavated at Jericho and Ai.

The guide agrees, and further informs us that this type of architecture with similar half towers has been found in Mesopotamia, and in drawings and carvings of the first dynastic period in Egypt.

Now the truck has stopped at the base of the citadel, and we pile out. Our lunch bags are left in an ancient bus near a tank of drinking water. We are instructed to return here at ten o'clock and eat our lunch under the shade of a canvas lean-to attached to the side of the bus.

Our group divides. Some prefer to work on the citadel. Most of us choose to excavate the Early Bronze city. Walking single file down a narrow rock-strewn path, we pass the tent of the Bedouin Sheikh, and furtively glance inside. Lying on the ground is a crying baby. The Sheikh seems to have very few possessions. We are astonished to find the tent is patched together with goatskin, burlap sacks, canvas, or any material that comes to hand. We avert our eyes as the women modestly cover their faces. When they think we are not looking, they boldly stare at us.

Now we have reached the Early Bronze city. Our guide explains that the rectangular stone foundations represent houses. He points to an opening in a long ridge of stone. "This is a doorway. See how the door was hinged on the left."

"How can you tell?" asks Sharon, a husky young girl from Colorado, who is spending her summer vacation on a kibbutz.

The guide points to a round depression in the stone, which

The Sheikh's tent and Bedouin women.

We are put to work on rock strewn ground.

Our tools consist of a small handpick, a trowel and a whiskbroom.

allowed an ancient doorpost to turn. He leads us to another house which has stone benches around the walls, and a stone work table in the middle.

"Have you any idea what these houses looked like?" asks Sharon.

"A clay model of a house was found in one of the rooms," answers our guide. "It had a flat roof and was painted with red stripes. Tonight after dinner you'll see slides of pottery, stone vessels, copper awls with bone handles, bone, shell, ivory ornaments, and clay animal figurines."

"How do you remember all these things?" asks Sharon.

"I run the slide projector," smiles our guide, as he leads us to some round structures which he says are foundations of granaries with the remains of grain in some of them.

At last we are put to work on some rock-strewn ground. A square about the size of an excavated room has been marked off by a string fence attached to low wooden pegs. Our tools consist of a small hand pick, a trowel, and a whiskbroom. We new volunteers are in a new section away from the Arab workmen. We eye our tools dubiously, and wonder how deep we can dig. Our guide sits down on the ground and loosens the soil very easily with his hand pick. Just a few inches below the surface are the rock foundations of the Bronze I city. When he has uncovered a portion of the foundation he brushes it clean with the whiskbroom and scoops up the excess soil into a rubber bucket. Suddenly he pounces upon a thin piece of brown stone and shouts, "This is a flint!"

"How can you tell?" we ask wonderingly.

"See how this stone has been shaped! Feel the edge! Careful—it's sharp; you can cut yourself. This is a stone knife!" Abruptly he leaves us to show the knife to the director.

In blind imitation we seat ourselves on the ground and begin to chop soil away from the rock foundations, brush them clean and scoop the excess soil into a rubber bucket. Bill, our guidebook authority, empties the rubber buckets into a wheelbarrow and hauls it to a dump pile.

Suddenly we are blinded by a whirlpool of dust. Sharon is burrowing deep into the ground like a rabbit. We tell her to stop choking us with dust.

"Wouldn't it be thrilling to find a whole pot or something?" She looks as if she were wearing black-face make-up. Suddenly she lets out a shrill squeal! She has struck something with her pick! Out of the soil she extracts a good-sized piece of broken pottery! She begins to brush away soil like a human steam shovel. Buried in the ground is a perfect pottery jar. Sharon has broken off part of the lip top.

We crowd around her, terribly excited at the sight of a whole jar buried in the ground. We are helping Sharon dig it out when our guide returns.

"Stop!" he shouts. "A jar like that has no archaeological value unless we photograph it in the ground!"

He brings the director to the site. She calls her assistant who photographs the jar at once. In awe we observe how tenderly they remove the soil so that the jar comes out whole. Handles on the body of the jar have broken off. The director inspects these as if they were precious stones, telling us, "Jars with ledge handles are so typical of this Early Bronze period. Some pots like this were found in First Dynasty tombs in Egypt, and Egyptologists called this foreign pottery from Palestine and Syria." She smiles. "Arad may have manufactured this pottery and exported it to Egypt."

Suddenly the stone foundations of the Early Bronze city have come alive for us. People really lived here who farmed, made pottery, did business with ancient Egypt.

Over fruit juice and sandwiches at ten o'clock lunch we dramatize our find to our friends who are working at the Citadel. They are not too excited because the Citadel is full of pottery sherds. They are much more excited about an Ashtoreth figurine which was discovered that morning. We learn that the Citadel was subjected to a number of sudden conquests, and the inhabitants fled leaving their possessions behind. Hundreds of pottery jars have been found on the successive floors of the Citadel, as well as a perfume distilling plant and a metal working industry. Many potsherds were covered with writing, a Hebrew script in the Israelite levels. The archaeologists called these sherds ostraca. Our guide tells us we will see pictures of these things at the lecture in the evening.

Before returning to our Bronze I city we stop at the Citadel to watch how carefully workmen uncover the Israelite fortress and

A ledge-handled vase.

a section of the sanctuary. Remains of six Israelite fortresses have been uncovered at Arad dating from Solomon in the tenth century B.C. to the end of the first temple in the seventh century. Walls built during the time of Jehoshaphat were four meters thick, the strongest walls of this period known in Palestine. The sanctuary appeared to be a large building with three adjoining rooms. The entrance faced east and the Holy of Holies to the west. This was the plan of Solomon's Temple described in the Bible.

Now we understand we must work carefully at the Bronze I city. As noon approaches we feel the heat. Gusts of a fresh wind from the ocean revive us from time to time. By two o'clock in the afternoon the sun, nearly vertical, drops its rays upon the excavation, obliterating every cool shadow. It is time to quit work.

We are tired after our first day's work, but not too tired to attend the selection of pottery sherds in the cool of the evening.

All pottery is brought to excavation headquarters, where it is sorted, labeled, and recorded. Next it is carefully washed, put out in the sun to dry in wooden boxes. In the evening the archaeologists select the best specimens from the boxes, which are filed along with other artifacts.

After the evening lecture we have a question and answer period. Bill asks, "The deeper you dig in the Tell the more you destroy. Will all the Roman, Greek, and Israelite ruins be gone? Shouldn't they be preserved so that everybody can see what happened in the past?"

The archaeologists explain that archaeology is destruction. Scientific excavation preserves everything through photographs, artifacts, and carefully written reports. If there were great works of art within Tell Arad they would not be destroyed.

So ends our first day on a dig.

Perhaps the next question is, What is the purpose of digging up the past? John Dewey, the American philosopher, has given this answer: "That which is past was once a living present, just as the now living present is already in the course of becoming the past of another present." In other words, from what we were, we know what we are. The archaeologist finds out what we were from man-made remains of past ages. The science of archaeology is only interested in the history of man's works, but to interpret them in time he needs the help of the geologist, the paleontologist, the physicist, the epigraphist, the historian. An isolated pottery bowl or inscription has no meaning unless it can be dated to a particular time in history. There are archaeological stages or periods which represent the materials out of which man made his tools. In this way we can trace his development in history. These Ages are: Paleolithic, Mesolithic, Neolithic, Chalcolithic, Bronze and Iron.

In Palestine, the Paleolithic or old Stone Age began about 250,000 B.C. when the world was covered with ice, and geologists call this time the Pleistocene. Men lived in caves during this period, existed by hunting, fishing, and food gathering. Their tools were made from chipped stone.

The Mesolithic, or intermediate Stone Age, is the name given to the time when the climate grew warmer, and the ice cap receded. This was about 10,000 years ago, and the climate approached our own, which geologists call the Holocene, or geological present. Great forests grew up in the temperate zones of Europe and America. Palestine was like a jungle sheltering huge elephants that are now extinct. But paleontologists have identified bones of these animals that have turned up in excavations. Man began to accustom himself to the change of climate and to build shelters outside of caves and domesticate animals like the dog.

About 7000 B.C. men had domesticated the cow, pig, sheep, and ass and grew plants for food like barley, millet, and hard-kerneled wheat. His tools were still made of stone. This is called the pre-pottery Neolithic, or new Stone Age.

The second stage of the Neolithic begins about 5000 B.C. when pottery was invented. People lived in small villages, farmed, and herded animals.

Men learned to smelt copper but used this metal mainly for ornaments. Stone continued as the material for tools in the Chalcolithic period (ca. 4000-3200 B.C.).

A new order of society was ushered in by bronze, an alloy of tin and copper. Supplies of these metals were far distant from the food-producing valleys in Mesopotamia and Egypt. The bronze makers were in a special class and kept their trade a secret. They became one of the first social classes. People who could afford to buy bronze tools, weapons, and armor gained power over the masses. Rulers arose along with classes of nobility and a priesthood. Bronze ushered in the beginning of urban life and saw the development of cities, classes, kings, gods, monuments, and writing.

There are three bronze periods:

Early Bronze:	3200 to 2200 B.C.
Middle Bronze:	2200 to 1550 B.C.
Late Bronze:	1550 to 1180 B.C.

Two thousand years after bronze was invented, people learned how to work iron and it became a boon to the mass of people because it was cheap and abundant. Bronze was the metal of kings, while iron was the metal of the common man.

The three iron ages are:

Early Iron:	1180 to 970 B.C.
Middle Iron:	970 to 840 B.C.
Late Iron:	840 to 330 B.C.

The following periods are all historical:

Hellenistic:	330 B.C. to A.D. 63
Roman Hellenistic:	A.D. 63 to 70
Roman:	A.D. 70 to 330
Byzantine:	A.D. 330 to 640

The later historical periods of the Arabs, Crusaders, and Ottoman Turks are not discussed in this book, but are archaeological periods in Palestine which are briefly referred to:

Islamic period:	A.D. 640 to 1073
Crusader's period:	A.D. 1099 to 1291
Islamic period:	A.D. 1290 to 1517
Ottoman conquest:	A.D. 1517
End of Archaeological periods:	A.D. 1700

A modern excavation is costly because it requires a large staff of specialists besides workers and equipment. Besides the archaeologists and their assistants, the staff consists of a competent architect, a surveyor, a photographer, as well as draftsmen, record keepers and epigraphists.

The equipment includes surveying and drafting instruments, good cameras, plenty of photographic material, digging equipment such as shovels, picks, hand trowels, jeeps, trucks, tents, and camping equipment.

Permission is needed to excavate sites. Modern excavations are usually carried on by governments, institutions, and foundations. The Arad excavation was sponsored by the Israel Department of Antiquities, the Hebrew University, and the Israel Exploration Society.

The Arad Development Project which is constructing a new city of Arad nearby financed a large part of the expenses.

Our work at Arad has ended, and we will leave the excavation in the morning. Now in the purplish haze of evening, outlines of hills emerge. Each hill has a fascination. We wonder—is it a mound? Is it a tell? Could a Biblical city be buried within that tell? Our feet crunch pottery and grind it into the sandy soil. We pick up a piece and observe it with a practiced eye. Byzantine pottery, of course—the light red sherds trimmed with ribbing litter the soil of Israel. We pick up a larger piece, which is circular and might be part of an oil lamp. In the fourth century A.D. lamps like this were the sole source of illumination. That was the time when Biblical archaeology began. If we could light this lamp perhaps it could lead us away from a twentieth-century excavation down the centuries to the Roman Empire in Byzantine times.

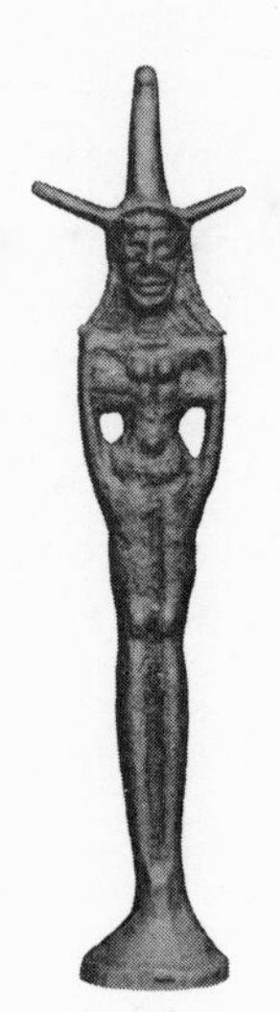

CHAPTER III
FOUNDERS OF BIBLICAL ARCHAEOLOGY

FROM THE LEGEND of a Roman queen to the Institute for Nuclear Studies at the University of Chicago may be translated into the years from A.D. 312 to 1950. This is the span of Biblical archaeology, if legends, travelers' journals, and observations of antiquarians are included. Biblical archaeology did not really begin until the nineteenth century. The scientific method was developed in the twentieth century.

This history is a story of adventurers, men and women who ventured into the neglected ancient world to search for the past. The degree of their success depended upon the kind of world they lived in; was it a time of war or peace?—a time of enlightenment or bigotry?—a period of recession or progress? These heroes of the potsherd set forth with pick and shovel to find the buried secrets of the past. Like St. George they fought dragons of ignorance but reached their goals through forces of knowledge. They are presented in their particular worlds, their historical setting.

A.D. 312 to 1800

In the year A.D. 312 the Roman Emperor Constantine the Great decreed Christianity the state religion of the Roman Empire. With Rome subjected to invading barbarians, the emperor abandoned the ancient city on the seven hills, and moved his capital of Constantinople in Asia Minor. This became the Byzantine Empire which from A.D. 312 to 1453 was the bulwark of Christianity and classical civilization.

Christianity spread rapidly through the Roman Empire which encompassed most of the civilized western world with territories from Scotland to the Sudan; from Portugal to the Euphrates. New Christians from all these territories wanted to see the land where Jesus lived and died. Pilgrims from all over the Roman Empire came to the Holy Land in droves. They arrived by land and sea. This was possible because a system of roads linked all Roman territories. There were no frontiers, no custom barriers; there was a single currency, a single law; educated people from the west spoke Latin, and those from the east, Greek.

Among the pilgrims was the aged Helena, mother of the Emperor Constantine. After a long, tiresome journey from Constantinople she was ensconced in a luxurious Roman villa at a city in central Judea called Aelia Capitolina. The hilltop villa had central heating, wall paintings, mosaics, and pergolas from which dangled ripened clusters of grapes. The Queen had a marvelous view of one of the newest and most modern of fourth-century Roman cities with a regular street plan, drainage, good water supply, imposing public buildings and temples, theaters, public baths, hotels, libraries and colonnades.

Aelia Capitolina bored the Queen. This city plan was duplicated all over the Roman Empire, even in far off Britain at a place called Londinium.

"Where is Jerusalem?" she asked.

"Jerusalem?" None of the Romans had the slightest idea. An official explained that three centuries had passed since the crucifixion. The Jews had revolted so many times that the emperor Hadrian made an end to Jerusalem and ploughed it under. In its place stood this beautiful, modern, Roman city of Aelia Capitolina. A portion of the temple wall remained from old Jerusalem. Every summer, on the anniversary of the destruction of the temple, Jews streamed in from everywhere, praying, weeping, lingering by the wall, even bribing guards to allow them to stay longer, for Aelia Capitolina was forbidden to Jews. The official shrugged his shoulders. He could not understand this attachment Jews had for their religion and their God.

According to legend, an old man appeared before Helena and said, "I know the place of the Holy Sepulchre."

He led the Queen to an excavated cave and pointed out the spot where Christ had lain. Three wooden crosses lay on the ground. "Those are the crosses of Christ and the two thieves who died beside him," said the old man.

The old man brought the Queen other relics of the crucifixion —two of the nails and the crown of thorns.

Helena brought these relics to her son, the Emperor Constantine, in Constantinople. Constantine was not really a Christian emperor. He issued an edict of toleration of Christianity, and was said to have been baptized on his deathbed; these relics had no religious significance for him. One of the nails he inserted into his imperial crown; the other he fashioned into a bit for his horse. Thus began the finding of relics by pilgrims and churchmen over the succeeding centuries.

Constantine honored his mother by building a number of churches on holy sites, sparing no expense to beautify them with mosaics, beautiful silk hangings, and golden vessels set with jewels. On the site of the temple of Venus in Jerusalem, Constantine built the Basilica of Anastasia, known today as the Church of the Holy Sepulchre. Over the centuries this church was rebuilt by the Crusaders, and again in 1808 after a fire. The Church of the Nativity was built in Bethlehem. In the seventh century A.D. a Mohammedan mosque called the Dome of the Rock was built over the site of the second temple of the Jews.

Until A.D. 644 when the Moslem Caliph Omar conquered Palestine, pilgrims from every corner of the Roman Empire converged on the Holy Land. Many of them landed at Caesarea, today a great tourist attraction of modern Israel, situated midway along the Mediterranean coast between Tel Aviv and Haifa. Caesarea plays a part in the history of early Christianity, for here Peter baptized the centurion Cornelius; Paul was imprisoned and, as recorded in Chapter 26 of Acts, held conversations with Agrippa. From Caesarea, Paul sailed to Rome. By the third century Caesarea had become a center of Christian learning under the famous scholar Origenes. His pupil was Eusebius, who by the beginning of the fourth century was bishop of Caesarea.

It is easy to imagine the scholarly Bishop constantly plagued by pilgrims who held important church offices in remote sections of the empire. They wanted to know the exact locations of towns and places mentioned in the Bible. Eusebius must have watched the pilgrims debarking from ships and falling into the clutches of guides who pretended to know everything, but did not even know the actual location of Bethlehem and Nazareth. These guides had camels and donkeys for hire; they hawked souvenirs and relics, and spun tall tales about legendary places which never existed. Thousands of pilgrims returned home with fictionalized descriptions of the Holy Land and brought souvenirs which were supposed to be the reed, spear, sponge, cup, and other items connected with the passion of Christ.

Eusebius realized that an accurate guidebook of Biblical place names was very necessary. He wrote such an accurate guidebook that archaeologists today identify sites from the Onomasticon, the name of the bishop's guidebook. He arranged the names in alphabetical order with an historical description of the events that took place there. About 300 names were listed as well as their distances to Rome and Damascus or a neighboring town. Arad was identified as "A village twenty Roman miles from Hebron." Despite the Roman occupation of Palestine in the fourth century, Hebrew place names were still being used.

The Onomasticon was translated into Latin by Jerome (ca. A.D. 340-420), known for his knowledge of Hebrew and Greek, and as a grammarian and rhetorician. This father of the Latin Church was for many years secretary to Pope Damasus in Rome. After the death of the Pontiff, Jerome removed to a monastery in Bethlehem. There he translated into Latin the Bible which is known as the Vulgate.

Early Christian scholars of the first three centuries of our era reconstructed a history of the world from the Old Testament. Finding no mention of the age of the world in the Book of Genesis, these scholars made their own calculation that man and the earth were created 6,000 years before their day. Eusebius and Jerome lowered the creation of the world to 4,000 years. This was the belief throughout the Christian world until the archaeological discoveries of the nineteenth century, and is even believed by some people today.

Jerusalem was considered the center of the earth. Jerome used

Ezekiel as his authority (Ezekiel 38:12): "That dwell in the middle of the earth," and (Ezekiel 5:5) "This is Jerusalem. I have set her in the midst of the nations, and the countries are about her." On this authority a thirteenth-century mapmaker drew a circular world with Jerusalem as the center.

From the time of Eusebius and Jerome to the nineteenth century, scholarly travelers visited the Holy Land and brought back interesting statistics and facts. Among them was Benjamin of Tudella who travelled from Spain to Palestine in A.D. 1160 to 1173. He crossed the desert from Palestine to Nineveh and Babylon where he saw a ruin of a ziggurat which he described as the Tower of Babel. Travellers between the sixteenth and nineteenth centuries visited Mesopotamia and described curious inscriptions they had seen on bricks. This caused the British East India Company to instruct its agent in southern Babylonia to find some of these inscribed bricks. In the year 1801 a shipment of inscribed clay tablets arrived at the East India House in London. When put on exhibition they aroused great interest among scholars and the general public who stood in line to observe these strange bricks. There was much murmuring and speculation as people asked, "What is the meaning of this strange writing? Is it something supernatural?"

A.D. 1800 to the present

Among the pigtailed men and women in great high caps, tight bodices and full skirts who came to view the inscribed clay tablets at East India House was his Majesty King George III. They respectfully watched their portly monarch strutting about in his great cocked hat, patting little children on the head, then listening to his band give a concert. Only a few of the gentry applauded him. The lower middle classes under the demagogue John Wilkes actually agitated against George III, not only because he had lost the United States, but also because they wanted a share of the prosperity brought on by the industrial revolution. The landed gentry were wealthy and happy in their pleasant and beautiful country houses. King George's palace was a model of an English gentleman's household. According to William Makepeace Thackeray, "It was early; it was kindly; it was frugal; it was orderly; it must have been stupid to a degree which I shudder to contemplate."

What happened to the lower classes? They migrated by the thousands to the Americas and Australia. During the nineteenth century not only the English, but people from all parts of Europe migrated to all corners of the world. Carlo Cipolla writes in his *Economic History of World Populations,* "They settled in the Americas and Australia. And they came to control Africa and Asia. The great exodus from Europe has been the most important migratory movement of the modern era, and perhaps the largest in all human history . . . There was something epic in a migration that saw Europeans spreading all over the world—building railroads, creating towns and harbors, opening canals, settling desert areas, bringing new lands under cultivation, and building factories, hospitals, missions, and universities."

These social changes, these migrations were brought about by the Industrial Revolution which began at the end of the eighteenth century when James Watt perfected a steam engine. Cotton mills, coal mines, blast furnaces, speeded up production by steam-driven machinery. There was increased production of food, textiles, housing, transportation and communication which caused a population explosion.

The Industrial Revolution is still going on in our time with automation and nuclear power. An archaeologist, Gordon Childe, used the term "revolution" to describe those times in history when mankind made a drastic change in living. The date of 7000 B.C. for the beginning of the Neolithic or Agricultural Revolution was determined from excavations of Kathleen Kenyon at Jericho. Carlo Cipolla defines the Agricultural Revolution as the period in history when men found the source of energy in plants and animals and the Industrial Revolution as the period when the source of energy came from science and machines.

The Industrial Revolution began in England and spread to France, and those two countries became the great powers of the nineteenth century, sending goods, gold, men and democratic ideas out into the world. They were colonizers, and made it possible for the English and French archaeologists of the nineteenth century to explore in safety the Bible lands we discuss in this book.

What was the rest of Europe like at the beginning of the nineteenth century? Russia was a huge sprawling slave state which extended from her western borders of East Prussia and Austria-Hungary across Siberia to the Pacific Ocean in the Far East. South of Russia was the Ottoman Empire whose capitol at Constantinople controlled the entrance to the Black Sea and blocked Russia from having a seaport on the Mediterranean. The Ottoman Empire spread over the Balkan Peninsula, Asia Minor, Palestine, Syria, Mesopotamia, Egypt, the Greek Islands and the coast of North Africa on the Mediterranean. This empire which we know today in Asia Minor as Turkey was disintegrating from internal corruption and despotism. Historians have called the Ottoman Empire the Sick Man of Europe, who should have died at this period. He was kept alive by Britain as a bulwark against Russia who was a threat to the passage to India. Austria-Hungary, too, was ready to fall apart, but like the Ottoman Empire survived until World War I. Prussia was a small rising power, Spain and Portugal were in a state of decline. The rest of continental Europe had been conquered by Napoleon Bonaparte, who had risen out of the French Revolution. He was a dictator but instituted a national system of education, endowed art and literature, and brought a new social order to his conquered subjects, benefiting in particular the Jews who were liberated from ghettos. Napoleon is of particular interest to our history for his invasion of Egypt, which brought about the discovery of a vanished civilization—Ancient Egypt.

The Rosetta Stone

In July of 1799 a French officer of engineers named Bouchard was sent with his company to Rosetta, a town in the western Nile delta. While the troops were tearing down an old wall, Bouchard noticed a stone built into the wall and covered with inscriptions. Bouchard, who could read Greek, observed the inscriptions were written in three different scripts, and rightly supposed they represented three versions of the same text.

Some of his companions who also read Greek agreed with him as he told them excitedly, "If these three scripts all say the same thing, it may be possible to decipher the hieroglyphics of the top inscription."

Bouchard immediately reported his find to headquarters, and received orders to bring the stone to Cairo. The young officer of engineers guarded the stone with his life as he and several soldiers carried it into a building with a sign reading "Institut National." Waiting to see the stone was Napoleon himself and a group of learned men whom Napoleon had taken with him on his expedition to Egypt. Their findings included many beautiful art objects which were now on display in the "Institut" before being shipped to the Louvre in Paris.

Two scholars, Jean-Joseph Marcel and Remi Raige, identified the middle inscription as a cursive form of hieroglyphic writing.

"What does it mean?" snapped the stocky conqueror of Europe.

"Sire, we can only read the Greek," answered the scholars.

Napoleon frowned, strode from one corner of the room to the other, put his snuff box to his nose. Then he began to gesticulate violently and shouted, "Send for the best lithographers in Paris to take impressions of this stone! Send copies to scholars of repute all over Europe—even the English! You, General Dugua," he turned to one of his aides, "commit two copies to the care of the Institut National of Paris."

Napoleon's order was carried out by two distinguished lithographers who covered the stone with printer's ink, and then placed upon it a sheet which they rolled with India-rubber rollers until a good impression had been taken. Scholars all over Europe received copies, but it was years before the mystery of the Rosetta Stone was solved.

Napoleon was so intent upon his conquest of Egypt, he left the French fleet anchored in Aboukir Bay and marched up the Nile. The English fleet under Lord Nelson boldly sailed into the bay, scuttled the French fleet and occupied Egypt. Under the conditions of the Treaty of Capitulation, the Rosetta Stone and several large Egyptian antiquities were surrendered to the English.

By the time the Rosetta Stone was deciphered in 1822 by a French scholar, Jean Francois Champollion, Lord Nelson had died a hero at Trafalgar in 1805, and Napoleon had died in 1821, a prisoner on St. Helena.

Champollion was helped by a list of alphabetic Egyptian characters, deciphered by an Englishman, Thomas Young, Champollion used these alphabetic Egyptian characters to decipher proper names. According to E. A. Wallis Budge, in his pamphlet for the British Museum, the decipherment of proper names provided a key to the system of writing, but could not have led to an understanding of the Egyptian language without the assistance of Coptic, Budge wrote, "Christian descendants of the ancient Egyptians are called Copts, a name which is only a corruption of the Greek, 'Aiguptos,' meaning Egypt. The translation of the Holy Scriptures, liturgies and other sacred writings which they made from Greek into their native tongue are written in the Greek script supplemented by seven characters derived from Demotic. [Demotic was the written script of ancient Egypt.] The knowledge of Coptic has never been lost, and its literature has always been available in manuscripts for study by scholars. Champollion, while still a youth in the early years of the nineteenth century, realized the great importance of Coptic for the purpose of Egyptian decipherment, and he studied it to such good purpose that he was able to identify very many of the Egyptian words which he could read with their Coptic equivalents. In his studies of the inscription on the Rosetta Stone his knowledge of Coptic enabled him to deduce the phonetic values of many of the syllable signs, and to assign correct readings to many pictorial characters, the meanings of which were made known to him by the Greek text on the Stone." Thus Champollion formulated the system for deciphering Egyptian hieroglyphics that is in use to this day.

The inscription on the Rosetta Stone is a copy of a decree passed by the general council of Egyptian priests at Memphis to celebrate the first anniversary of the coronation of Ptolemy Epiphanes in the spring of 196 B.C. The original decree was made in Greek. The Demotic and hieroglyphic versions were made from it. The old picture writing was used for all ceremonial and state documents intended to be seen by the public from 3000 B.C. to Roman times. During the Ptolemic period Demotic or cursive writing was still used.

Cuneiform Writing is Deciphered

In the winter of 1851, a British soldier, Major Henry C. Rawlinson, appeared before the Royal Asiatic Society with a translation of a cuneiform text. Since the days of George III the British were familiar with the wedge-shaped writing on clay tablets. Huge bas-reliefs from Nineveh and Khorsabad in Mesopotamia had been shipped to the British Museum by an adventurous young diplomat turned archaeologist named Henry Austin Layard. In fact he had written a best-selling book about his adventures excavating, and his name was on every tongue. Rawlinson was unknown. No one had ever heard of a mountain near Behistun, Persia, where an inscription had been carved on the face of a cliff twenty-five centuries ago by the Persian King Darius.

The applause of the Society to Rawlinson's presentation was polite but skeptical. How could they be sure this soldier had found the key to the decipherment of cuneiform. A Reverend Edward Hincks from Ireland had already published a list of Akkadian characters. The French scholar Jules Oppert was known to be making progress in this field.

The bulldog in Rawlinson made him stand firmly in his shoes. He acknowledged that he had found the work of other scholars helpful. He had spent fifteen years working on this project. As a young lieutenant with the army of the East India Company he had first become interested in the sculptured cliff. At first the figures fascinated him. The life-sized figure of King Darius stood with his left foot placed on the prostrate form of Gaumata, the leading rebel. The king grasped a bow with his left hand, and his right hand was lifted toward a winged disk with the head of Ahura Mazda. On either side of the king were his attendants, while behind Gaumata was a procession of rebel leaders, roped together by their necks. A later addition to the group was Skunka, a Scythian wearing a pointed cap. Beneath the sculptured panel were many inscriptions. Rawlinson decided to copy them and translate them into English. Risking his life he climbed up the cliff to a rocky ledge where he could stand and plainly see the inscriptions. There were three of them. By 1844 he had copied the bottom inscription. To copy the topmost lines, he had to stand on the last step of a ladder, steadying his body against the cliff with his left arm which held his notebook. His right arm was free to write. According to his memoirs, the inscriptions were so interesting that he lost all sense of danger.

He left Behistun for three years, but returned in 1847 to copy the last inscription.

"You can't climb to that top inscription," warned the goatherders who grazed flocks near the mountain. "Nobody has ever climbed up there."

"I'll climb up there if you pay me enough," volunteered a young Kurdish boy.

Rawlinson hired the boy but reminded him that the inscriptions were 345 feet from the ground, and the highest point to which a man could climb was 100 feet. Darius had removed all stone beneath the inscriptions, making the face of the cliff smooth and slick in the hope that his inscription would never be mutilated or debased. Nevertheless, nature had eroded it with wind, rain, and time, so that parts of it were erased.

By means of ropes attached to a wooden peg driven into the rocks, the boy managed to reach the top text. Rawlinson contrived a swinging seat such as painters use. There the boy sat as Rawlinson directed him how to make a paper cast of the inscription. Now Rawlinson had a copy of the top Akkadian text, and the bottom text in old Persian. The middle Elamite text was not deciphered until 1948 by Professor George Cameron of the University of Michigan. Rawlinson first deciphered the Persian part of the inscription, and from this finally read the cuneiform.

The British public who were deeply interested in the Old Testament voiced their opinions. The Holy Scriptures made no mention of cuneiform writing, and that was proof enough that Rawlinson did not know what he was talking about. Besides, if this writing was so involved, how could the Assyrians read it?

At last W. H. Fox Talbot, respected for his discoveries in photography, attempted to decipher cuneiform himself and made the following suggestions to the Royal Asiatic Society by letter: A copy of the same text should be given to three or four leading cuneiform authorities for translation. Appoint a reliable committee to compare them.

This appealed to the English sense of justice and fair play, so that none other than the Dean of St. Paul's Cathedral was a member of the committee.

Copies of an inscription of Tiglath-pileser I were sent to Henry Rawlinson, Dr. Hincks, and Dr. Jules Oppert. The three men made identical translations of the inscription. The committee certified that cuneiform writing could be read and translated into a modern language.

Queen Victoria knighted Henry Rawlinson for his achievement. Now all the thousands of clay tablets stacked in the basement of the British Museum, to say nothing of the huge alabaster bas-reliefs on exhibition, could be read. The most surprised person was Sir Henry Austin Layard, whom the Queen had knighted for digging up all these antiquities at Nimrud and Nineveh. Layard's most famous discovery was the Black Obelisk of King Shalmaneser III, which was sculptured on four sides. The inscription identified a prisoner at the feet of the king as Jehu, king of Israel.

"Jove!" Layard must have tugged his well-trimmed beard, adjusted his mid-Victorian waistcoat, and gasped discreetly, for he had no idea back there in 1846 at Mosul that he was actually digging up a portrait of a king of Israel.

Sir Henry Rawlinson called Layard's attention to the fact that the kings of Israel, like Jehu, Menahem, Pekah, and Hoshea, actually lived and were historical characters according to the inscriptions.

Layard at the age of thirty-four was a retired archaeologist, and devoted the rest of his life to diplomacy and politics. He died in 1894, but is remembered as the discoverer of the most significant remains of the four Assyrian kings: Ashurbanipal II, Shalmaneser III, Sennacherib, Tiglath-pileser III.

French scholars at the Louvre were delegated to decipher inscriptions on the Assyrian marble sculptured panels, stone bas-reliefs, wall paintings, and thousands of inscribed clay tablets that came from the palace of Sargon II (ca. 721-705 B.C.) at Khorsabad. They had guessed this was Sargon's palace when they commissioned Paul Emile Botta, the consular agent in Mosul, to turn archaeologist and excavate there. Mosul was a textile center that produced the paper-thin muslin or mousseline so popular for women's dresses. This Assyrian king, Sargon II, is mentioned only once in the Bible (Isaiah 20:1) : "In that year Tartan came unto Ashdod when Sargon the king of Assyria sent him."

The deciphering of Egyptian hieroglyphics and Mesopotamian cuneiform carried the good Victorians back a few thousand years before Christ. The shock of the century came in 1859, when they discovered their Stone Age ancestors.

Stone Age Man?

It was the year 1859. The Aberdeen meeting of the British Association for the Advancement of Science was in session. An announcement was about to be made. Newspapermen were anxious, but not half as anxious as a composed middle-aged Frenchman, Jacques Boucher de Crévecoeur de Perthes (1783-1868), an amateur antiquarian, who had presented proof that man lived at the same time as extinct animals. Hugh Falconer, a British paleontologist and friend of Boucher de Perthes, was sure the decision of the society would be favorable since his colleagues, Joseph Prestwich, John Evans, and Charles Lyell, agreed with him. Lyell had announced his acceptance of Boucher de Perthes' evidence before the society, and showed it harmonized with researches on British soil.

Boucher de Perthes did not raise his hopes. "I found thousands of flint stone tools in the terraces above the Somme River near Abbeville, France. Twenty-one years ago I defended my thesis before the local Société Impériale d'Emulation at Abbeville."

"What happened?" asked Falconer.

Boucher de Perthes answered sardonically, "Practical men disdained to look; they were afraid; they were afraid of becoming accomplices in what they called a heresy, almost a mystification; they did not suspect my good faith; but they doubted my common sense."

"After your treatise in 1846, *De L'Industrie Primitive,* your worst antagonist, Dr. Rigollot, examined the sites from which you secured tools and admitted you were right," said Falconer.

"Yes," said Boucher de Perthes. "But those who disagreed shouted louder. Some self-styled authorities insisted the hatchets were no older than Roman times. Some of them insisted the tools had sunk to Pleistocene depths by their own weight; others stated the tools were not made by men, but had been shaped by glacial or volcanic action."

In the wake of a burst of applause, Charles Lyell emerged through the doors of the meeting room, his face aglow with smiles. "They've accepted your thesis, Monsieur. Come, they are waiting for you to speak!"

Boucher de Perthes told the learned audience that stone tools were not merely knives and hatchets, but a language, an art, and social customs. His discoveries created a revolution in thought, a flood of light on prehistory, a new perspective on chronology. Now the history of man went back into the Pleistocene or glacial period, 200,000 B.C.

Some years later books, such as Huxley's *Man's Plan in Nature,* Lyell's *Antiquity of Man,* and Darwin's *Descent of Man,* used this evidence to present new theories regarding the origin and history of man. The religious and intellectual worlds were shaken to the depths, never dreaming that in the 1920's prehistoric people would be found in Palestine who would be potential ancestors of homo sapiens. We shall discuss this in detail in Chapter IV. Robert H. Lowie wrote in *The History of Ethnological Theory,* "As homo sapiens was zoologically at the peak of the animal kingdom, so Western Europe in 1870 marked the goal of civilization." A. L. Kroeber wrote in his Anthropology, "It became common practice in the older anthropology to 'explain' any part of human civilization by arranging its social forms in an evolutionary sequence from lowest to highest . . . In these schemes we of our land and day stood at the summit of the ascent."

L. H. Morgan, a nineteenth-century anthropologist, projected such a theory of cultural evolution. Evidently Morgan's works were read by Karl Marx and formed the basis of his Socialist classic written by his literary executor Friedrich Engels: *The Origin of the Family, Private Property and the State.* They traced the socialistic order from savagery, through barbarism, and beyond the industrialized capitalistic societies of today. Conversely, at the end of the first World War, Lothrop Stoddard wrote *Rising Tide of Color* and Madison Grant wrote *The Passing of the Great Race* using these theories of cultural evolution to achieve political ends. The seeds they planted flowered in Nazism. This is relevant to our history, for although scientific scholars have long discarded these theories, they are still being taught and learned in our day.

If the discoveries of Boucher de Perthes had profound repercussions in the social sciences, the geographical discoveries of Edward Robinson in Palestine were a positive help to archaeologists in locating Biblical sites. At that time Palestine was controlled by the aggressive Egyptian, Pacha Mehemet Ali.

Early Surveys of Palestine

The broad-shouldered Americans looked like bearded patriarchs as they rode single file into the hill country of Judea in the year 1838. Edward Robinson felt like a patriarch, for all his life as a student of Biblical geography and a professor at the Union Theological Seminary in New York he had dreamed of this ride. Now as he followed his friend Dr. Eli Smith who was a missionary at Beirut, Syria, he practiced his Arabic, and Eli Smith laughingly corrected his pronunciation, saying, "You can't seem to lose that Bostonian accent, Ed."

"When we reach the next settlement, let me speak to the natives and see if they understand me," said Robinson.

They came to a village called el Khalil. Robinson was sure this was the site of ancient Hebron, or Mamre, where Abraham pitched his tent beneath the oaks (or terebinths) (Gen. 13:18 and 18:1). Dirty children with sore eyes were playing on bare hard ground in front of a mud brick house. Some elderly men were smoking water pipes in the shade of a roofed porch. Robinson and Smith dismounted and gave the reins to their only servant Ahmed, who was leading the supply donkeys, one of which he rode. Robinson addressed the men in good scholarly Arabic. They regarded him blankly. Then Eli Smith who could speak their dialect inquired for the village scribe. All the men understood him and almost in concert told him there was no scribe in this village but at the next village west, Taffuh, there was a very learned man.

"Taffuh!" Robinson extracted a small Bible from his pocket and thumbed through to the place he wanted (Joshua 15:52): "Beth-tappuah, 'house of the apple tree,' listed as one of the cities belonging to Judah. You see, Eli, how the Arabic place names follow the Hebrew names," said Robinson. "Tappuah in Hebrew, and Taffuh in Arabic. I'm positive all these modern Arabic place names have their roots in ancient Hebrew names in the Bible."

The scribe at Taffuh was also mullah, or the teacher and interpreter of Islam law and dogma at the local mosque. When the Americans arrived they heard the chant of young voices from the courtyard of the mosque as young boys learned passages from the Koran by word of mouth. The mullah was surprisingly rugged and young for a learned scholar. At first he regarded the Americans suspiciously, for he thought they were English. He had never seen Americans before.

Over small cups of strong sweet coffee in a cool room of the mullah's mud brick house, the Americans learned that the mullah had been an instigator of a revolt against the Egyptian dictator in 1834, which had been crushed. The tenant farmers of the Hebron mountains and Nablus were nothing more than serfs. Now the outlook for freedom was worse than ever, in fact hopeless. The only hope the mullah had was education. How could he educate the young with no books in Arabic?

Then Eli Smith told the mullah that before he came to Syria he had been in charge of the missionary printing house in Malta. Since he had been in Beirut he had devised an improved font of Arabic type, which would insure printing type of one size and style. He planned to go to Leipzig, Germany, and personally supervise the casting of this type. Then perhaps the children of Palestine could learn to read and write, for the mission at Beirut would print text books.

Then the conversation turned to the location of Biblical sites. The mullah gave the Americans directions to places in his area and gave them names of people farther north who might aid them. Robinson and Smith gave the mullah gifts of candles and charcoal in appreciation of this valuable information. These gifts were luxuries among the poverty-stricken peasants of Palestine.

For two and one-half months Robinson and Smith rode over the hills and trails of the Negev, the Judean Hills, the Jordan valley. At night they always camped above the wadis to escape flash floods. Their supplies consisted of rice, biscuits, coffee, tea, butter, dried apricots, a tent, compass, telescopes, measuring tapes, two old muskets and a pair of pistols which they never used, the Bible in Greek and Hebrew, and five of the most important travel books in Palestine.

Both men kept journals and scientifically recorded the temperature four times a day, sunrise, sunset, time of arrival at each point of interest, directions of important places, prices of supplies, and notes about customs of Arab tribes. Within two and one-half months Robinson had material from which he later published three volumes. He vastly improved existing mapmaking and located scores of Biblical towns whose sites were completely unknown.

While in Jerusalem he measured, surveyed, and explored the Siloam tunnel which King Hezekiah built while Sennacherib was besieging Jerusalem.

Robinson made a second trip to Palestine in 1852. The Royal Geographical Society of London awarded him their Patron's Gold Medal. Dr. Eli Smith realized his ambition of bringing to Syria the first Arabic type for printing books. He made possible the printing of Arabic text books. Learning did not filter down to the illiterate masses who were medieval in their thinking and who organized their life on earth according to their religious concepts. The Protestant missionaries who founded the American College in Beirut and the Jesuit University of St. Joseph did much to revive the old literature and purity of classical Arabic. Turkish censorship hampered the development of the press in Syria and Palestine. All efforts toward reform met with opposition from orthodox Moslems, who resented any concessions of equality for the Christians.

The Crimean war was fought over the protection of the holy places in Palestine. France had guarded the Roman Catholic shrines and Russia demanded the right to guard the Greek Catholic shrines. Great Britain was allied with France and Turkey against Russia who was defeated. In 1860 there were clashes between the Moslems and Christians on Mount Lebanon in Syria, and France with the consent of Britain occupied Syria while Britain took over Crete. Into this inhospitable atmosphere came C. R. Conder, a British army engineer, to make a survey of Palestine in 1865. He had been sent by the Palestine Exploration Fund, who stated as their purpose: the accurate and systematic investigation of the archaeology, topography, geology, and physical geography, the manners and customs of the Holy Land, for Biblical illustration.

Conder's memoirs tell how flies swarmed over them, and some of the men died of fever. Unfriendly Arab tribes tried to stop their work by attacking them with stones and clubs. Hardly a member of the surveying party escaped injury. Despite these hardships Conder and his men surveyed all but 1,300 miles of Palestine and this later was completed by Lord Kitchener.

In 1880 British surveyors had produced an accurate map of Palestine with 9,000 names accurately located on an area of 6,000 square miles of western Palestine. Plotted to a scale of one inch to one mile, this map extended over twenty-six sheets, and when joined together the map measured 7 by 13 feet. The surveying party published seven large volumes of memoirs with much useful information.

Semitic Studies in the Nineteenth Century

Soon after the French occupation of Syria in 1860, Ernest Renan, a French philologist and historian, was sent by Napoleon III to excavate in Syria, particularly Phoenicia. Soldiers of the French army served as excavators for Renan, and he even had a French naval vessel to transport him to the different sites along the Syrian coast—Ruad, Byblos, Sidon, and Tyre.

Renan was anxious to explore Phoenicia, and was familiar with Phoenician script which had been deciphered in the eighteenth century by Abbé Jean Jacques Barthelémy. On the island of Malta a four-line Phoenician inscription had been found with a Greek inscription below it. Malta is 1,200 miles from the coast of Phoenicia in Syria, but the ancient seafaring Phoenicians had settlements all over the Mediterranean. Abbé Barthélemy, through his knowledge of Hebrew and Greek, determined the meaning of the Phoenician letters and read the text.

Renan failed to discover anything in Syria. He did make a great contribution to archaeology after he returned to France in 1867. He instituted a plan for the French Academy of Inscriptions to publish all known Semitic inscriptions in a collection known as Corpus Inscriptionum Semiticarum. The first corpus was published in 1881, with a photograph of each text, which was transcribed into Hebrew, then translated into Latin with a full commentary. Three large volumes contain over 5,000 Phoenician inscriptions. A second part contains Aramaic inscriptions and texts. A thousand South Arabic and over 5,000 North Arabic inscriptions and texts have been published. The Hebrew inscriptions have not yet been published, but the work still goes on and is a most important source for students of Canaanite culture.

The Beginning of Scientific Chronology

In the year 1890 Flinders Petrie was a famous Egyptologist with ten archaeological volumes to his credit. Then the Palestine Exploration Fund asked him to excavate in southern Judah for the Biblical city of Eglon. The British public had become so intensely interested in the relation of the Old Testament to antiquity that small contributions of ordinary people amounting to £1,110 poured into the treasury of the society. This great interest was evoked in part by the opening of the Suez Canal in 1860, the occupation of Egypt by Britain in 1882, and the discovery through archaeological excavations of ancient Egyptian civilization.

For weeks Petrie was detained in Jerusalem waiting for the slow wheels of Turkish bureaucracy to turn on the green light which would give him permission to excavate in Palestine. When the "go signal" at last came, he immediately started south, a one-man expedition with a donkey man to carry his equipment and supplies. The trails up and down the Hebron mountains were dry, hot, and solitary in the late spring. But every evening as the sky streaked red and purple and the golden sun sank into the sea, the wind blew fresh sea air into his face and refreshed him for another day of searching for the mound that might be ancient Eglon. At last he found a hill that corresponded to his map and explored it for three days, but only found a Roman village. He moved on to other sites, tested them, and found nothing.

View of Tell el Hesi across grainfield.

Eastern side of Tell el Hesi where Petrie found the layers of pottery.

On April 17th, 1890, he came to Tell el-Hesi. This mound rose out of a yellow grain field like a square-topped pyramid. As Petrie stalked through the grain he realized it was almost ready for harvest. The field ended at a dry river bed called Wadi-Hesi, which Petrie crossed to reach the mound. He climbed and measured the mound which was about 100 feet high above the fields and extended about 200 feet each side of the top. Then he looked down the eastern side of the mound which was a jagged cliff sloping at about a 45-degree angle. Petrie began to climb down this cliff which was so steep he almost lost his footing if he had not grabbed onto a ledge. There he sat down to rest and observed that this eastern side of the mound had evidently been washed away from flash floods which the winter rains had sent racing down the Wadi. Petrie pulled what he thought at first was a loose red rock out of the cliff. The minute he felt the object he knew he had found pottery! Petrie began to scrape the cliff with his knife and realized it was built up in layers of pottery, and the pottery in each layer was different! Could it be possible he was looking at a thousand years of history on one hill? He decided to terrace each level and get out the pottery.

Petrie found workers six miles away. He began the work by terracing each level, and kept each level of pottery separately. Some Egyptian objects turned up in certain levels, which were a great help in dating the Palestine pottery of the same level. By linking Egyptian chronology to this project, he made a chart dating the various levels. Later on, Petrie's dating of Egyptian dynasties was proved too high for Tell el-Hesi, and the dates were revised. Many years later in excavations at Jericho some copper objects were found that corresponded to a copper axe and other weapons that Petrie had found at the lowest level of occupation. This dated Tell el-Hesi at 2600 B.C. rather than 2000 B.C.

For six weeks Petrie directed his one-man excavation, using thirty men as laborers and women with baskets to carry away the soil. He set his pick men a fixed distance up the slope, each one cutting a step in the hill. Pottery types varied with the altitude. Types of pottery found in the top five steps might be rare in the next five, and absent in the one below. Petrie assumed that a style of pottery was used as long as a town was inhabited. If a style was found by one pick man and not by the man below him, Petrie knew this style was short-lived. This short-lived pottery was valuable for dating, because it showed a margin of error. Petrie worked out a chart on which every piece of pottery on the hill was assigned its proper place in historical sequence.

For the first time Palestinian archaeology had a sound method of dating excavations. The work was closed down by the workers going off to harvest their crops. Petrie returned to Egypt where he preferred to work, and did not work in Palestine again until 1927.

Another important discovery in 1887 was some clay tablets inscribed with cuneiform writing at Tell el Amarna, about 200 miles south of Cairo. The tablets are known as the Amarna letters and were the correspondence between the Egyptian kings Amenhotep III and Ikhnaton and the governors of Egyptian-controlled cities in Palestine, Syria, and other parts of Egypt's Asian empire. These letters will be discussed later.

The most important excavations before World War I were those in 1910 under the Americans G. A. Reisner and Clarence S. Fisher at Samaria, sponsored by Harvard University. These men developed the method of excavation now in use throughout the Near East, using a careful, meticulous method of surveying, photography, drawing, and recording as well as digging.

Nineteenth-century civilization in search of art, trade, and colonies fell apart in World War I. Science, inventions, art, music, and learning survived. So did some of the false prophets who brought on World War II. After World War I the Ottoman Empire was no more. Palestine was proclaimed a homeland for the Jews and was given to Great Britain acting as a mandatory for the League of Nations. Syria was handed over to France on a mandate basis.

Modern archaeological excavations begin from this period. In 1920 and 1921 William F. Albright, director of the American School for Oriental Research, made a survey of Samaria and Galilee. He identified sites by means of pottery sherds. During the 1920's many new sites were placed on the map by Albrecht Alt from Germany and Dominican Père H. Vincent from France.

Nelson Glueck made a survey of Transjordan from 1932 to 1947. He had gone to Palestine as an assistant to Albright. From pottery sherds collected in bags and carefully labeled, he recorded evidence from more than 1,000 ancient settlements. His notes on his travels, drawings, and photographs of pottery fill five large volumes. He also made a complete survey of the Negev in southern Israel.

In 1923 Pierre Montet, with the help of French soldiers who were put at his disposal by the French high commissioner, General Maxime Weygand, found a site at Byblos that has become a mine of information for contacts between ancient Syria and Egypt from inscriptions, coins, and artifacts.

The sensational discovery of the 1930's was at Ras Shamra, the modern Arabic name for the town of Ugarit. One day, while an Arab peasant was ploughing his field near the north Syrian coast, his plough struck a large stone. It belonged to a tomb that contained pottery. This turned out to be a cemetery belonging to a low-lying mound, and the most important Canaanite site yet found. The site was excavated by Claude F. A. Schaeffer. Within a week Schaeffer found a library of ancient Ugarit with inscribed tablets, seventy-four bronze weapons and instruments, including five axes with inscriptions. For eleven campaigns until World War II Schaeffer worked on this site. After the war he started again and in 1956 had completed his twentieth campaign of this inexhaustible site.

Some tablets inscribed with an unknown cuneiform script were sent off to Paris to the scholar Virolleaud, who prepared them for publication in the archaeological journal *Syria*. Fifty of these texts in the unknown cuneiform text were sent to other scholars. In less than a year and a half after the tablets were taken out of the ground, the script had been deciphered by M. Virolleaud, with help from Professor Hans Bauer at the University of Halle in Germany, and Père P. Dhorme at the Ecole Biblique in Jerusalem. This achievement stands in strong contrast to that of scholars of the nineteenth century, and was due to the French publishing so promptly and to international cooperation in their translation.

The scholars called this new language Ugaritic from the place where it was found. Ugarit was revealed as a city at the crossroads of the world, where people came to trade from all over the Mediterranean. Ugaritic was the language of the Canaanite Bible, a literature about half the size of the Hebrew Book of Psalms.

All archaeological excavations stopped with World War II, but were resumed with the peace. The sensational post-war discovery was the Dead Sea Scrolls.

In 1950 another method for dating excavations was discovered by Professors J. R. Arnold and W. F. Libby of the Institute for Nuclear Studies at the University of Chicago. They published some dates by testing ancient organic material for carbon 14. All living organisms contain carbon 14. The rate at which their radioactivity is lost has been established. The surviving activity of ancient organic matter is measured and in this way its age calculated. There is always a margin of error of several hundred years. For example, in 1948 some land snails were found at an excavation in Iraq in a pre-pottery level. These were found to be 6707 years old, with a margin of error at 320 years on either side of the central date. In Egypt, a slab of wood from the tomb of a Vizier named Hemaka who lived in the first dynasty was dated between 3100 and 2800 B.C. By carbon 14 the date obtained was 2933 B.C. with a margin of error at 200 years. Carbon 14 is proving to be a good source for dating periods before 3000 B.C. Pottery sherds are still the most reliable in historic periods.

With this brief background of the development of archaeological science, and the history of important discoveries, we will follow Biblical history as viewed from the different archaeological periods.

CHAPTER IV

WE ARE FROM WHAT WE WERE

Prehistory in Palestine
50,000 B.C. to 10,000 B.C.

THE PREHISTORY OF Palestine has the same unique quality that is characteristic of Biblical history. It has a firstness—the Biblical, where man found God through righteousness; the prehistoric, where the neolithic or agricultural revolution began. Further research may reveal earlier beginnings of man as a settled farmer, but at this writing, the discoveries of Kathleen Kenyon at Jericho are accepted.

The first discovery that prehistoric man dwelt in Palestine came in 1925 when Tureville Petrie, a young Englishman, discovered the frontal part of a skull, along with some stone tools, in a cave in Galilee. This cave can be seen today. All that is needed is sturdy tires on the car and a sharp eye to see the small sign that leads to wheel tracks across a grain field, then down a bank to an ancient, boulder-strewn riverbed called Wadi Mugharet ez Zutteiyeh. It is possible to inch up the wadi by driving inside the wheel ruts of other cars which obviously use this as a road. The narrow canyon does encourage symptoms of claustrophobia and fear of being drowned in a wall of water sent down the canyon by a flash flood. This is hardly possible in Palestine's dry summer season. It is difficult to turn back, once the wheels of the car are imprisoned in the road ruts, and huge rocks block an easy turn.

The car moves forward between steep canyon walls, roofed overhead by blue sky streaked with clouds.

Suddenly a pink cliff ahead is smirched with black holes! The canyon has widened! Mountains on either side are riddled with dugouts! These are the prehistoric caves. Here the Wadi is sandy and level, providing good parking space. A gash in the hill directly in front of the car reveals an archaeologist's trench. A steep climb about a quarter of the way up the mountain leads to the gaping entrance of a large cave.

Inside, the stench of guano and dead bats is overpowering. A huge cavern whose vaulted ceiling reaches heights far in excess of a Gothic cathedral connects with pitch black rooms and corridors in the heart of the mountain. Millenniums of campfires have encrusted the walls with soot. It is best to contemplate the prehistoric home of man in Palestine outside his door in the fresh air, unless, of course, the stench is bearable.

This would have been uncomfortable in Pleistocene times when rain fell almost continuously in Palestine. An ice age covered Europe, but the glaciers did not come down this far. A jungle grew up in this part of the country from the wet, tropical climate. Monster rhinoceroses, hippopotami, elephants, and cave oxen roamed over the land. Fossil bones of the animals have been found all over Palestine, along with stone tools at the same level.

It is easy to imagine Palestine man standing at the door of his cave watching the rain. He was a mixed-type Neanderthal man, between thirty and forty years old, about five feet six, tall for a prehistoric man. His face was rugged, with large eyes under the continuous ridges of his brow, wide nose, chin underdeveloped. He stood erect and walked with a human gait. How do we know all this? He was similar to fossil men found in Croatia in the Balkan Peninsula, and some fossils of a child, men and women found in a cave near Mount Carmel. He lived by hunting, fishing and foodgathering. His tools were made by selecting a smallish, smooth cobblestone, which he recognized as a flint. Grasping the stone with his powerful hand, he struck it against a boulder, or hit it with another rock, and knocked off flakes of stone. The core of the flint served him as a hand axe or pick. He chipped it so that the round side fit the palm of his hand. The pointed end, when thrown, could penetrate, crush a skull, or break limbs. This was

View of prehistoric cave in Wadi el Mughara.

a useful tool to split wood, hack limbs from trees, butcher game, and roughly dress hides. It is possible he discovered some of the thinner flakes of stone were sharper, and he used these as knives. One of the sharp little flints, when attached to a long pole, made a good hunting spear. It is possible Palestine man hunted and fought his enemies with a spear, because in the skull of one of his relatives at Mount Carmel was a spear wound.

Wadi el Mughara (Cave Canyon) at Mount Carmel is not much more than an hour from the cave in Galilee. The home of these relatives of Palestine man was plainly marked by a sign on the highway south of Haifa. The dirt road meandered around a banana plantation, then turned for a short distance into some foothills. Before us round black cave entrances dotted the mountain like black windows in an apartment house. A baronial arched door with two windows hewn out of the living rock marked the imposing entrance to the main cavern. Here in 1931 and 1932 Dorothy Gerrod and T. D. McCown found twelve skeletons, preserved in breccia or a mass of debris and chipped stone, that revealed a people of mixed race between Neanderthal man and homo sapiens or modern man. They explained this mixture of races by the geographical position of Palestine as an international bridge. In his book *Man and His Works,* Melville J. Herskovits wrote: "These remains are particularly important, for it was their discovery in the late 1920's that forced the conclusion that the transition from Neanderthal to homo sapiens was gradual, and not due to the clash of two species that resulted in the extinction of the less advanced."

10,000 B.C. to 7,000 B.C.

About 10,000 years ago when the climate changed to the geological recent, or the climate we live in, the cave dwellers of Palestine adopted a new way of life. Dorothy Gerrod first discovered people of this period in rock shelters in the eastern slopes of the Judean hills near the Wadi en-Natuf. She named them Natufians, after the Wadi. Remains of the Naftufians were also found in the Carmel caves. All these people buried their dead under the floors of their caves. They made fine little flake stone knives with a straight edge and a crescent-shaped back called lunates. They fished with bone harpoon points and bone fish hooks. The most exciting tool of the Natufians was a stone tool shaped like a sickle, an agricultural implement. These were set into a slotted bone handle carved with animal heads. There were also stone picks or hoes used to break up ground before sowing grain.

At first the sickles may have been used to gather wild grain, for Palestine and Syria are known to be the home of wild grains. W. F. Albright writes, "It follows that the earliest Natufians whom we can trace were already cultivators of grain, though doubtless in the most primitive stage of hoe-culture (Hackban). They were thus food producers as well as food gatherers."

These people kept dogs. A fine canine skull was found that appeared to be a domesticated descendant of a jackal. Their graves show they wore necklaces of bone, pierced teeth, and shell, and even wore shell headdresses from such ornaments found at the sides of skulls.

There were remains of Natufians over such a long period of

time that archaeologists divided them into lower, middle, and upper Natufians, according to their implements. Dorothy Gerrod had no idea when their culture ended. Even though they were the earliest known food cultivators, they still hunted and fished.

The Natufian mystery was like all archaeological mysteries; an excavation was only a clue to prehistory. In 1958, this mystery was solved.

Kathleen Kenyon was directing an excavation at the ancient Tell of Jericho in 1958. This mound is on the outskirts of modern Jericho, which is an oasis in the desert. The Tell is about 70 feet high and covers about 10 acres. At the foot of the Tell is a perennial stream which is the water supply for modern Jericho, and was the reason for the many cities that built up the ancient mound. The source of the stream is an underground river fed by the rains in the mountains of Judea. Jericho, which is 900 feet below sea level, has heavy winter rainfall, but the land is scorched and dried up by the summer heat. The desert soil is very fertile when irrigated. The irrigated fields around this stream at Jericho are very productive.

Our story is concerned with Miss Kenyon's excavation in the middle of the Tell of Jericho. There, from 1929 to 1936, John Garstang had discovered the first pre-pottery Neolithic urban culture. In other words, this was the first town before the Neolithic or agricultural revolution when men made pottery. Miss Kenyon began excavating in the middle of the Tell, expecting to find another level of walls. There were no walls, just floor levels, bounded by slight humps, which were the remains of hut-like houses. The excavators kept digging—more floors—more humps—down—down—for 13 feet until they hit bed rock! They had reached the bottom of the Tell! What could this mean?

At the opposite or north end of the Tell they had also hit bed rock. The basic limestone was in its natural state, covered by a layer of clay about a foot thick. The clay had been removed from most of the area by men, exposing the basic limestone. At the south end of this excavation a large rectangle of clay like a platform had been enclosed by a stone wall. Wooden posts had been set in the wall at intervals. Two large stone blocks had been built into the wall, and holes 2 feet by 6 inches had been bored right through them. They were obviously post holes, for flag poles or totem poles. This enclosed clay platform was scrupulously clean, but the rock surface outside the wall was covered with debris and rubbish. Miss Kenyon surmised this clean platform area was a sanctuary or some kind of holy place.

Sifting through the debris, a crescent-shaped Natufian stone knife turned up! A bone harpoon head like those found at the levels of the Lower Natufians at Mount Carmel was found! There was charcoal strewn about, which showed this building had wooden beams which burned down. What a fortunate catastrophe for the archaeologists! Charcoal could be tested by carbon 14, for dating. The carbon 14 dating of this charcoal was 7800 B.C. plus or minus 210 years. Miss Kenyon wrote: "This dating has for the first time given us a relatively fixed point for the transitional stage in man's development into a civilized being."

Putting all the clues together what did it mean? The sanctuary may have been established by Natufian hunters from the Carmel caves who came to the stream at Jericho because it was also a water hole for game. They built the sanctuary at the source of the stream which gave them nourishment and worshipped it. We know from the Caves of Carmel that they practiced agriculture. But the humps under the 13 feet of hump and floor deposits showed that people were living beside the spring of Jericho for a long time. They were living in one spot but their huts were like those of nomadic hunters. When did they start to live in solid houses?

Let us climb up through the 13 feet of floors and humps, to find an example of the first Palestinian house. It was round like a hut and had a domed roof, also a projecting porch which was entered by steps or a sloping ramp. The walls were built of hand-molded flat bricks shaped like backs of pigs (hog-backed). In some of the houses wooden posts strengthened the roof; in others, twisted tree branches strengthened the walls. These solid brick houses expanded into a town estimated at ten acres, in contrast to the small area of the 13-foot deposit. The Natufian hunters had settled down into an established community. Eventually it was defended by a solid, free-standing wall six feet, six inches wide and twelve feet high. Inside the wall was a watchtower reached by twenty-two steps. It must have taken a long period of cultural growth until the Natufians could build such a town. How long was determined from charcoal timbers taken from some burned-down mud brick houses that stood against the tower wall. Carbon 14 gave a dating of 6850 B.C., plus or minus 210. Dorothy Kenyon writes: "The descendants of the Neolithic hunters who had established their sanctuary by the spring of Jericho had, therefore, made a remarkable progress. In the course of a period which carbon-14 evidence suggests is about a thousand years, they had made the transition from a wandering to a settled existence."

The change came about through the development of agriculture and the domestication of animals. Jericho provided the date for this first great economic revolution—7000 B.C.

7000 B.C. to 4000 B.C.

Men are given credit for domesticating animals, women for inventing pottery through accident. They may have covered a basket with clay to make it waterproof. It fell into a hot fire and turned into pottery.

Animals came to cultivated fields looking for food. A farmer may have made a pet out of a lamb or a kid. Then he noticed that if he allowed animals to graze off the rubble of his harvest he had a better crop the next year. The calf, lamb, kid, little pig willingly stayed on his farm as long as he fed them. When they became cows, sheep, goats, and hogs, they depended on him for food. He was compensated when they produced young, and he had twice as many animals. It was much easier to raise meat than hunt it. He added a new food to his diet, milk.

The farmer who lived by the stream at Jericho conquered some engineering problems, building irrigation ditches, channels into fields, and sluice gates to close off channels when another farmer needed water. Irrigation of lands created the necessity for laws in a community of farmers and persons in control, so that no one farmer would monopolize all the water or take fields and animals away from his neighbor. Peoples of the irrigated lands developed law codes early in their history. They had to unite together and build defense walls against enemies. Such communities were greatly concerned with the territory of their herds and fields. At Jericho, in such a town, were found clay figurines of animals. These people lived in square houses with courtyards and plastered the floors and walls of their houses. Beneath the floor of one of these houses were found skulls. The lower part of the skull was plastered and moulded into a likeness of a human face. Shells were inserted into the eye sockets. These people made a large variety of stone knives and tools and some well-made white limestone bowls. A saddle quern was found. This is a slab of stone on which another stone is pushed back and forth to grind grain, like the Mexican metate.

About 5000 B.C. a group of villages stretched around the northern part of the Fertile Crescent. From the Iranian foothills to Egypt were a chain of Neolithic villages, all making pottery. This pottery was built up by hand, and dark, bag-shaped bowls have been found in many sites.

4000 B.C. to 3200 B.C.
Chalcolithic Age

Chalcolithic comes from chalcos, meaning copper, and lithos, meaning stone.

This is a transitional period with great development in settled life, pottery-making, and the use of copper as a material for axe-heads, arrow-heads, and ornaments.

Teleilat el Ghassul, excavated by Pontifical Biblical Institute between 1929-38 in the Jordan Valley opposite Jericho, showed that in the Chalcolithic period pottery was being made in a great variety of shapes and was well decorated. During this period, the potter's wheel was invented. At first a mat was used as a table, which the potter could turn together with the clay, while shaping his pot with both hands. Mat impressions have been found on the bottom of pots of this period. Eventually a wooden disk was used which developed into the potter's wheel.

The pottery decoration gives us a picture of the times. Pots were trimmed with clay imitations of the ropes by which jars were carried. Little clay houses like those in which people lived were found in graves filled with bones, so that the dead would have the same shelter they knew in life. These are called ossuaries.

A copper smelter was found in an underground dugout at Abu Matar near Beersheba, by M. Parrot. The copper was melted in open fireplaces, then refined in crucibles. Scattered about was slag and ore, as well as copper mace heads, pins, rings, ornamental cylinders, and handles. Analysis of the metal showed it came from the mines of Arabah Aravali which are about 60 miles distant.

Palestine had many settlements during this transition period. Chalcolithic villages have been discovered all over Israel in recent years.

3200 B.C. to 2200 B.C.
Early Bronze Age

How bronze was discovered is not known. It was used in Mesopotamia by 3500 B.C., in Egypt by 3000 B.C. Bronze is an alloy of tin and copper, which makes it harder than copper, but bronze melts more easily and casts better.

As we approach 3000 B.C. when history was being written, let us consider the achievements of men before this date, according to V. Gordon Childe: artificial canals and ditches; the plow; harnessing of animal motive power; the sailboat; wheeled vehicles; the potter's wheel; orchard husbandry; fermentation; the production and use of copper; bricks; the arch; glazing; the seal; the solar calendar; writing and numeral notation; bronze.

Now that we have reached the Early Bronze period and historical times, let us look at the two great civilizations—Sumerian-Akkadian-Babylonian and Egyptian.

CHAPTER V

THE MESOPOTAMIAN BACKGROUND

THE SUMERIANS WERE the founders of a great cultural heritage which was carried on faithfully for thousands of years by the Semitic peoples of Western Asia.

Sumer in the Early Bronze Age (ca. 2900 B.C.) lay in the wide flat delta of the Tigris and Euphrates Rivers near the Persian Gulf. This land was made up of city states. Some of them were: Ur, Nippur, Lagash, Erech, Eridu, and Kish. These cities were really temple states whose land belonged to the gods who were represented by the king of the city. Through a temple corporation, the land was leased to the farmers. This developed into a large business enterprise. Consequently business was held in high repute in Sumer. To keep track of all the business transactions writing was devised, and laws were enacted that all business dealings should be in writing.

Every city had its special god who had a house which he shared with the other gods at the top of a huge temple called a ziggurat. This was a huge staged tower built of mud bricks and had recessed tiers which looked like those of an immense wedding cake. All the business and life of the town centered about the ziggurat.

In the city of Ur the patron god was the Moon Ninnar. Ur like all the rest of the Sumerian cities based its economy on mud and water—they had no other natural resources like wood and metal. Their myths and legends tell the stories of how they drained the marshes, dyked the water and built canals which became the highways on which they travelled in small boats. This irrigated land produced an abundance of barley and emmer wheat, good grassland for cattle and sheep, apple orchards, date groves, vineyards, and vegetable gardens. They invented the potter's wheel and were the first to spin wool and weave woolen garments. Their building material was mud bricks, which at first were hand-made and later were form-made. The Sumerians piled up massive walls and buttresses with these mud bricks, and even invented the true arch which was later copied and used by the Romans.

Mud or clay provided the material for writing. The clay writing tablets were made of the finest and cleanest clay that the spring flood waters deposited on the banks of the Tigris and Euphrates Rivers. Perhaps for this reason the clay tablets have remained intact, buried in the ground all these thousands of years, while the buildings disintegrated into dust. The Sumerians worked out their speech in cuneiform or wedge-shaped writing which was done on wet clay with a wooden stylus. The writing became wedge-shaped because the scribe could not make curves in clay with any speed. He used horizontal, vertical, and wedge-shaped strokes. The development of cuneiform writing can be seen from the early tablets, which are almost word signs or ideographs, to the late cuneiform which is almost alphabetical. When the Akkadian Sargon I conquered Sumer in about 2360 B.C., Akkadian became the language of the country, but the religious texts were copied by scribes in Sumerian. This was a great creative period in literature and science and continued until the Babylonian period under Hammurabi (ca. 1728-1686). Cuneiform writing was used by the early Assyrians (ca. 1234 B.C.), by the historical Persians under Cyrus and Darius (ca. 549-515 B.C.), and even by the people of Ugarit on the Syrian coast (ca. 1500 B.C.) who had devised an alphabet but wrote on clay with cuneiform strokes. Because scribes scrupulously copied the old texts and kept business records, archaeologists have been able to dig up the huge libraries of clay tablets, collected by the Assyrian kings, and those of Ugarit, Mari, and Nuzi. From these libraries we have come to know their literature and laws.

The excavations of the tombs at Ur by Leonard Woolley and the University of Chicago have revealed something of the life in ancient Ur. From the Sumerian poem "Gilgamesh and Agga," translated by S. N. Kramer, we find that the Sumerians had one of the most ancient of political assemblies. In this poem the city of Kish has demanded the submission of Erech, and the poem reads:

> "The Lord Gilgamesh before the elders of his city
> Put the matter . . . . seeks out their word."

From this we can assume the power of the king was not completely absolute. If we followed a king and queen of Ur as they visited a ziggurat, we would find they rode in a square cart with disk wheels pulled by a team of oxen, followed by many slaves and courtiers. The king wore a gold helmet and had blue lapis lazuli ornaments in his beard. His bronze sword had a gold filigree handle. The queen wore a necklace of lapis lazuli and gold ornaments in her hair.

When they entered the huge, brick-paved courtyard of the ziggurat they smelled the savory odors of a sacrifice which was also the main meal of the morning when a large bull and bullock were offered to the deities, Anu, Ontu, Ishtar, and Ninnar, "who dwell in the topmost stage of the temple-tower." The altar was heaped with loaves of bread, honey, date wine, cucumbers, apples, grapes, and milk. The king and queen partook of the sacrifice, and the king prayed to the Moon-God:

> "O Sin, O Ninnar glorified one . . .
> Who furnishes light for the people . . .
> To guide the dark-headed people aright."

Next the royal pair observed the business dealings of the temple corporation. The courtyard was crowded with people who wanted land transfers and farmers who were selling their produce and cattle. After the deals were made, the people went into the counting room where rows of scribes were either sitting or squatting down beside little mounds of clay from which they fashioned tablets of all sizes. For instance, a farmer who brought in an offering to the temple was given a receipt written on a small piece of clay, and the scribe wrote down a memorandum of his offering on another small piece of clay which he placed in a basket. At the end of the week these memorandums were entered on a large tablet and tabulated. Archaeologists found these huge clay tabulations recording a month's or even a year's business transactions. Naturally the king glanced over the weekly tabulation, then watched a scribe write out a contract for the sale of land. The two contracting parties signed the tablet by impressing their cylinder seals in the wet clay. Merchants carried their seals on a string around their necks. The scribe made a duplicate of the contract on a thin piece of clay which was also signed and witnessed, then applied over the original like a pie crust. The scribes were so skillful with these covers they never stuck to the bottom copy. They were a safeguard in case of a dispute where the top cover might have been changed. A judge made a decision by breaking off the cover and reading the original.

The king was particularly interested in the most profitable department of the corporation where poor people borrowed barley, or smiths and merchants borrowed copper and silver, at interest.

The king and queen really wanted to see the astrologists on the top floor of the tower to hear their fortune. On the way up they looked in at the school for scribes on the second floor and the weaving factory on the third, where hundreds of women spun woolen thread and wove cloth for the temple.

The king and queen were very respectful toward the wise men of Sumer who occupied the top floors. Here were the mathematicians who not only figured out measurements for properties but worked out a complete system of weights and measures. These were subsequently adopted all over the ancient world and are the source of the 12's and 60's and their multiples that remain in our hours, minutes, ounces, and degrees. Later on, the Babylonians developed zero and place value numeration. The Mesopotamian astronomers applied their mathematics to astronomy. They were the first to identify the planets, plot their wanderings, set up a zodiac, and make predictions of potential eclipses. They were mainly interested in the changeable aspects of the heavens and adapted themselves to the irregularities of the lunar calendar. The Egyptians, as we shall see in the next chapter, sought fixed repetition and devised the solar calendar. Over a period of a thousand years the Sumerians and Babylonians achieved genuine

Courtesy Louvre

Hammurabi, King of Babylon, standing before the seated God Shamash, at the top of stela inscribed with laws.

scientific results, and the Hellenistic sciences, which we will investigate later, built upon them.

These vast Mesopotamian business enterprises required law codes. Now we leave our Sumerian king and queen. Our next consideration is the five law codes which have been discovered by archaeologists:

Ur-Nammu of Ur	—	2050 B.C.
The Laws of Eshnunna	—	2000 B.C.
Lipit Ishtar of Isin	—	1850 B.C.
Code of Hammurabi	—	1700 B.C.
Hittite Code	—	1500 B.C.

A huge monument of black diorite, which stood seven feet, five inches high and was inscribed with the 250 laws of Hammurabi, was found at Susa by the French archaeologist, Jacques de Morgan. A small section of the prologue, as translated by Theophile J. Meek, reads:

"at that time Anu and Enlil named me
to promote the welfare of the people,
me Hammurabi, the devout, god-fearing prince,
to cause justice to prevail in the land,
to destroy the wicked and evil,
that the strong might not oppress the weak,
to rise like the sun over the black-headed (people)
and to light up the land."

The laws of personal injury are of particular interest, for there is a similar collection in Exodus 21:12-27.

"If a son has struck his father, they shall cut off his hand."

"If a seignior has destroyed the eye of a member of the aristocracy, they shall destroy his eye."

"If he has destroyed the eye of a commoner, or broken the bone of a commoner, he shall pay one mina of silver."

"If he has destroyed the eye of a seignior's slave or broken the bone of a seignior's slave, he shall pay one half of his value."

This was the law of the land at the time of the Hebrew Patriarchs. There were three classes of society: the class of free men, or feudal lords; commoners; slaves. The rights and responsibilities of each were determined by laws. About two hundred Hittite laws, inscribed in cuneiform writing on clay tablets, were found at Boghazkoy in Asia Minor. These laws were contemporary with the time of Moses.

Now let us see what these law codes have in common with Biblical law. They are all collections of particular rules. Many of the Israelite laws are casuistic or "if" laws. If a bull gores a man—that bull shall be stoned. This is the style of most Near Eastern laws.

The lex talionis, the law of retaliation, appears in all these codes: life for a life, eye for an eye, tooth for a tooth, etc. Bodily mutilation as punishment by this law was common in the time of Hammurabi. It was used to excess by the Assyrians, who take their place in history, along with the Aztecs and the Nazis, as the most cruel and sadistic of people. Hammurabi's code provides fines as punishment for bodily mutilation. This was true of the Hittite and Biblical laws. Fines were imposed in place of retaliation among the Israelites except in special symbolic cases (Deuteronomy 25:11-12). Crucifixion is not known in the Old Testament and was not one of the punishments used by the Israelites.

There is a similarity between Hittite treaties and Israel's apodictic laws, which lay down commands and prohibitions in the second person future. Exodus 20:17 states: "Thou shalt not covet thy neighbor's house; thou shalt not covet thy neighbor's wife, nor his man servant, nor his maid servant, nor his ox, nor his ass, nor anything that is thy neighbor's."

The Hittite treaty also had imperative statements: "You shall keep the land which I have given you and shall not covet any territory of the land of Hatti."

This resemblance of the Covenant between Israel and God to a Hittite treaty is very striking. God was a party to the Covenant, because it was His law that governed the relations of men with one another as well as their relations with God. The people had undertaken an obligation to obey God's laws, which also instructed them how to live.

Other similarities can be seen in the Eastern laws, inscribed on tablets of clay or carved on stone and placed in a sanctuary in the presence of the gods. The Ten Commandments were inscribed on two tablets of stone, placed in an Ark or box and kept in the Tabernacle or Sacred Tent. The pact made at Shechem between God and the Israelites in the time of Joshua was written on stones and preserved in the sanctuary.

The Hittites ordered the text of their treaties to be read before the vassal king and his people periodically.

Biblical law reads, Deuteronomy 31:12, "Gather the people together, men, women, and children, and the stranger that is within thy gates, that they may hear, that they may learn and fear the Lord your God, and observe and do all the words of the law." The Israelite laws were regularly read to the people.

Of all these ancient law codes only the Israelite law remains until this day. Why has it endured and become part of Christianity and Mohammedanism as well as Judaism?

Biblical law provided Israel with a common heritage which bound them to keep the covenant of leading a moral life and worshipping one God. The moral responsibility is individual. No God, no king can be a substitute for the individual conscience. Man must conquer his own instincts of aggression and self-destruction. Biblical law is not a collection of placid maxims but thunderous admonitions. Leviticus 26:3 gives hope: "If ye keep My commandments," God will send rain, peace, victory over enemies. Leviticus 26:14 warns, "If ye will not hearken unto Me," the land will not produce and will be conquered by enemies. Always man is told, "And thou shalt love the Lord thy God." This is the crux of the matter. The man who truly loves God is humane and feels compassion for his fellow creature. Père De Vaux has emphasized the humane aspect of the Biblical laws, as opposed to the Eastern laws. Flogging is limited to forty strokes, "Lest the bruises be dangerous and your brother be degraded." Leviticus 19:33 tells us, "if a stranger sojourn with thee in your land, ye shall not do him wrong." Deuteronomy 15:11 says, "Thou shalt surely open thy hand unto thy poor and needy brother in thy land."

The Eastern codes are all laws of kings, made for the purpose of enforcing their authority. The king governs, and the judges decide according to justice and truth. Biblical law is the law of God and is to be kept through duty and devotion, and kings and judges are not excepted. This difference is seen in all the parallel stories from Mesopotamia, particularly the story of the flood, which is in the Gilgamesh legend and closely parallels the Noah story of Genesis.

The discovery of the Mesopotamian flood story was revealed on December 3, 1872, when George Smith, an assistant repairer at the British Museum, made a most astounding announcement to a distinguished audience of scholars and theologians. "A short time back," said Smith, "I discovered among the Assyrian tablets in the British Museum an account of the flood, which, under the advice of our president, I now bring before the Society of Biblical Archaeology. On reviewing the evidence it is apparent that the events of the flood narrated in the Bible and the inscription are the same and occur in the same order."

"Incredible! Fantastic! The story of Noah and the flood, written on cuneiform tablets in the library of Ashurbanipal II which had been dug up by Austin Layard back in the 1840's. Absolutely fantastic!" said the nineteenth-century audience.

On the cuneiform tablet, the hero was not Noah but Utnapishtim. The story of the flood was part of a great epic poem called "Gilgamesh," one of the literary masterpieces of Sumer and Babylon. George Smith had been deciphering cuneiform tablets for ten years at the Museum. He had made some discoveries and published them in the *Athenaeum*. One day he was copying cuneiform signs on half a tablet and read a reference to a ship resting on the mountains of Nisir. When this was followed by an account of the sending forth of a dove and its finding no resting place and returning, he knew he was on the track of something sensational! Was this the Babylonian story of the flood? He searched through thousands of fragments of clay tablets. Gradually he found other portions of the same story, pieced them together, and realized how similar this was to the Biblical story of the flood. He guessed about fifteen lines were missing.

After the London *Daily Telegraph* printed the story of a Babylonian flood story, so much public interest was aroused that the newspaper offered George Smith a grant of 1,000 guineas to reopen the Nineveh excavations and find the missing pieces of the flood story.

By May of 1873 Smith was at Nineveh, digging. Within a week he found the missing portion, which was seventeen lines. George Smith telegraphed the good news to his sponsor. The editor,

Courtesy Louvre

Gilgamesh.

satisfied that the archaeological publicity stunt had worked out so well, told Smith to come home. Fortunately, the British Museum sponsored Smith in a second season where he recovered over 3,000 inscriptions. In 1876, he began a third expedition. He suffered an attack of dysentery and died at the age of thirty-six. He was buried at Aleppo in Syria.

Since George Smith discovered the flood story, fragments of the Epic of Gilgamesh have been found all over the Middle East. Recently a shepherd walking over a mound of debris at the excavation of Megiddo in Israel picked up a cuneiform tablet. When it was read it contained forty lines of the Gilgamesh Epic.

The Epic of Gilgamesh, according to the American poet William Ellery Leonard, revolves about "sex love, combat, friendship, adventure, valor, loyalty, the mountain, the field, the forest, the wild beasts, the sea, the storm, the gods, the mysteries of birth and death." Gilgamesh seeks immortality but ends his quest knowing all men must die.

Gilgamesh, a legendary king of Uruk, has a friend named Enkidu, who is his faithful companion in many adventures and hardships. Enkidu dies, and this is the portion found at Meggido:

> "Stricken is Enkidu, one day,
> Enkidu's suffering on his bed increases,
> A third day, a fourth day, . . .
> Stricken is Enkidu on his bed!
> At length he called Gilgamesh and said to him,
> My friend . . . has cursed me!
> Not like one fallen in battle shall I die."

After Enkidu has died, Gilgamesh mourns him, and it is reminiscent of David's lament over Saul and Jonathan.

> "He who with me underwent all hardships
> Enkidu whom I loved early,
> Who with me underwent all hardships,
> Has gone now to the fate of mankind . . .
> Day and night I have wept over him."

Courtesy Israel Department of Antiquities

Fragments of Gilgamesh recently found at Megiddo.

In II Samuel, 1:26-27, King David laments:

> "Jonathan upon thy high places is slain.
> I am distressed for thee, my brother Jonathan;
> Very pleasant hast thou been unto me,
> Wonderful was thy love to me,
> Passing love of women,
> How are the mighty fallen,
> And the weapons of war perished!"

George Smith not only discovered the flood story but cuneiform tablets with the story of the Creation. He published a book on these tablets, which caused a great religious controversy. There are seven tablets of the Babylonian story of the Creation which begin in the primordial time with the divine pair, Apsu, the fresh water, and Tiamat, the salt water. Nothing else existed.

James B. Pritchard has matched the accounts of the Babylonian creation story with that of Genesis in his work, *Archaeology and the Old Testament*.

Babylonian	*Genesis*
1. Primordial watery chaos Tiamat and Apsu.	1. Existence of unformed earth and the deep.
2. Birth of Marduk, "Sun of the heavens."	2. Creation of light.
3. Fashioning of the sky from half the body of Tiamat.	3. Creation of the firmament of the sky.
4. Squaring of Apsu's quarter (the earth).	4. Gathering the water together to form the earth.
5. Setting up of the constellations.	5. Creation of lights in the firmament.
6. Making man for the service of the gods.	6. Creation of man to have dominion over animal life.
7. The divine banquet.	7. Resting of God on the seventh day.

A clay tablet was found in Egypt which was a school exercise for a scribe learning to write cuneiform, the language of diplomacy in the second millennium. This concerns the "Fall of Man."

The tablet begins: "To him he had given wisdom. Eternal life he had not given him." The story is about a man Adapa who was created by Ea, the patron god of Eridu. Adapa's task was to provide bread and fish for Ea. One day the South Wind capsized Adapa's fishing boat. Adapa cried out, "South wind! I will break thy wing!"

Just as he said this with his mouth, the wing of the south wind was broken. For seven days the south wind did not blow on the land.

The great god Anu called his vizier and asked, "Why has the south wind not blown over the land these seven days?"

The vizier told the god what Adapa had done.

Anu cried, "Fetch him hither."

The sly Ea advised Adapa to put on mourning clothes and said, "When they offer thee the bread of death, thou shalt not eat it. When they offer thee the water of death, thou shalt not drink it."

When Adapa reached heaven he followed Ea's advice and refused the bread and water.

Anu looked at him and laughed, "Come now, Adapa! Why didst thou neither eat nor drink? Thou shalt not have eternal life! Ah, perverse mankind!"

Adapa told how Ea commanded him not to eat or drink.

Anu commanded, "Take him away and return him to earth!"

The unhappy Adapa realized that Ea had tricked him out of his chance to be immortal. This story has been compared to the Garden of Eden story, (Genesis 3:22), "Lest he put forth his hand, and take also of the tree of life and eat and live forever."

The quest for immortality is the theme of the Gilgamesh epic. The story of the flood is told to Gilgamesh by Utnapishtim to explain his immortality.

"The gods said to Utnapishtim:
Man of Shuruppak, son of Ubar-Tutu,
Tear down this house, build a ship.
Give up possessions, seek thou life.
Forswear worldly goods and keep the soul alive!
Aboard the ship take thou the seed of all living things.
The ship that thou shalt build,
Her dimensions shall be to measure.
Equal shall be her width and her length. . . .
Like the Apsu thou shalt ceil her."

The poem describes the building of the ship:

"The little ones carried bitumen,
While the grown ones brought all else that was needful.
On the fifth day I laid her framework.
One whole acre was her floor space,
Ten dozen cubits the height of each of her walls,
Ten dozen cubits each edge of the square deck.
I laid out the contours and joined her together.
I provided her with six decks,
Dividing her thus into seven parts.
Her floor plan I divided into nine parts.
I hammered water plugs into her.
I saw to the punting poles and laid in supplies."

The loading of possessions, animals, family, craftsmen is described:

"Whatever I had I laded upon her;
Whatever I had of silver, I laded upon her;
Whatever I had of gold I laded upon her;
Whatever I had of all the living things I laded upon her.
All my family and kin I made go aboard the ship.
The beasts of the field, the wild creatures of the field,
All craftsmen I made go aboard."

He describes the storm. A black cloud rose up from the horizon,

"Inside it Adad thunders.
Six days and six nights,
Blows the floodwind as the south-storm sweeps the land.
When the seventh day arrived,
The flood carrying south-storm subsided in the battle
Which it had fought like an army.
The sea grew quiet, the tempest was still, the flood ceased.
I looked at the weather; stillness had set in,
And all of mankind had returned to clay.
The landscape was as level as a roof.
I opened the hatch and the light fell upon my face.
I looked about for coastlines in the expanse of the sea;
In each of fourteen regions,
There emerged a region-mountain.
On Mount Nisir the ship came to a halt. . . .
A fifth and a sixth day, Mount Nisir held the ship fast, allowing no motion.
When the seventh day arrived,
I sent forth a dove,
The dove went forth but came back; . . .
Then I sent forth a raven.
The raven went forth and seeing that the waters had diminished,
He eats, circles, caws, and turns not round.
Then I let out the four winds
And offered a sacrifice.
The gods smelled the sacrifice, crowded around Utnapishtim,

and found that Ea the great god had told Utnapishtim
to build
the ark to save mankind. They bless him.
Hitherto Utnapishtim has been human.
Henceforth Utnapishtim and his wife shall be like unto
us gods."

In the story of Noah the building of the ark is practically the same. According to Genesis 8:3, the rain stopped after a hundred and fifty days, and the ark rested on Mt. Ararat, which is in Anatolia; and this story may have come to the Hebrews through the Hittites or the Hurrians. Noah sent out a dove and a raven and made a sacrifice to God, who made a covenant with Noah. Genesis 9:13 says, "I have set My bow in the cloud for a token of a covenant between Me and the earth, And it shall come to pass when I bring clouds over the earth, and the bow is seen in the cloud, that I will remember my covenant . . . and the waters shall no more become a flood to destroy all flesh."

In the Babylonian story, Utnapishtim offered a sacrifice to the gods, who smelled the sweet savor of the sacrificial meal and collected about him like flies. The god Enlil was angry that Utnapishtim and his family escaped the flood. But Ea interceded, arguing that it was not just to have the righteous destroyed with the sinners. Then Enlil blessed Utnapishtim and his wife with immortality.

Here can be seen the unique difference between Yahweh and the Babylonian gods. Yahweh is the god of the covenant who made and kept promises and who looked after his people. It must be remembered that the Book of Genesis as we know it was written about the fifth century B.C. This is approximately 1500 years later than the Gilgamesh poem. The stories in Genesis were handed down orally at first, written perhaps many times, before they were put into the literary form we know. The great Biblical writers used the stories of creation, Adam and Eve, and other stories in Genesis to teach the oneness of God, as well as moral precepts.

The great Semitic culture of Mesopotamia was part of Israel's background, along with the other peoples of Western Asia. When the monarchy of Israel emerged in the year 1000 B.C. the creative period of Mesopotamia had been over a long time, but not dead. Scribes kept the ancient learning alive, copying the poems and stories on clay tablets, for the huge libraries of the Assyrian monarchs.

CHAPTER VI

THE EGYPTIAN LEGACY

THE ROLE OF EGYPT IN THE Old Testament is that of the oppressor from whom the Israelites escaped into the desert. There they made their covenant with God and emerged a new people with a purpose.

At the time of the Exodus (ca. 1290-1224 B.C.), in the reign of Rameses II, Egypt was reaching the end of almost 2,000 years of a civilization that for Egyptians was happy, sensuous, given to good living, fearful of death, and one in which they comforted themselves by dealing in symbolism and magic. A. L. Kroeber sums up Egypt's achievements as: the solar calendar, the forms of their art including both the hieroglyphic characters and animal headed deities; political unity of the whole land under the king-godship; preoccupation with death, and attempts to achieve an almost bodily afterlife with the Osiris myth of the "dying god," or rather "revivified god" type. They invented bellows for metal working, faïence and glass and were the first to weave flax into linen garments. The donkey and cat came from Egypt.

Egypt was cut off in Africa and self-contained in the Nile valley. This great river rises in the high mountains of Abyssinia and travels north. In North Africa which is Egypt, the Nile is a long blue ribbon of water piercing the yellow ochre desert and banding it with green. The fertility of the Nile Valley depends upon a flood which deposits soil from distant mountains in

Abyssinia upon the hot desert sands. This flood in turn depends upon the southwest monsoon, which is a periodic wind from the Indian ocean, breaking upon the mountains of Abyssinia. This wind will normally reach any given place at the same point in each of the earth's journey's round the sun. In other words, the wind reaches a given point on the same day in each solar year. All the Egyptians had to know in order to predict the flood was the length of the solar year and reckon such a year from one observed flood as a starting point to the next observed flood.

Since farming in the whole Nile Valley depended on the annual flood, the Egyptian astronomer who could predict the flood was either a god or magician to the people.

An unknown Egyptian astronomer or a group of astronomers observed that the flood came about the same time every year. Over a period of fifty years, the flood came every 365 days but always on the 365th day. They divided the 365 days into ten months of thirty-six days each, with five extra days each year. This was out of gear with the real seasons and could not be used as a guide for farmers in their agricultural work. After a century the royal officials corrected the errors by observing the star Sirius (Sothis in Egyptian), which in the vicinity of Cairo is the last star to appear on the horizon before dawn obscures all the stars at the flood season. This was the date fixed for New Year's day, when the signal was given to the farmers to prepare for the flood.

It has been suggested that the ability to predict the flood was kept secret in order to make the pharaoh a god who, by his magical powers to predict the flood, controlled the seasons and crops.

The calendar was introduced under Menes, who unified Egypt about 2900 B.C., or the Early Bronze Age. This was the Old Kingdom which lasted until about 2200 B.C., and the great age of the Pyramids and the Sphinx of Gizeh. The Memphite Empire reached its apogee from about 2840 and 2680 B.C. under the kings Cheops, Khephren and Mykerinos who built the great pyramids and extended the influence of Egypt as far as Byblos in Phoenicia.

The Memphite portrait statues in diorite almost reproduce the personality of kings, queens, courtiers, and working people. Later, in the Middle and New Kingdoms, Egyptians developed

Courtesy Louvre

Life-like portrait statue of an Egyptian scribe.

the post and lintel architecture with columns. This style of architecture was used in Phoenicia and Solomon's Temple, and was further developed in Persia and Greece. The Phoenicians copied Egyptian statues and statuettes which are so full of delicacy and charm. The ivory carvings of cherubs from Samaria are Phoenician copies of Egyptian art. Even their gods with the head of a ram, jackal, or hawk are imaginative, decorative, and completely unreal in their symbolism.

Egyptian art influenced all of western Asia. This is especially true of the Sphinx, reproductions of which have been found among the Hittites, and whose likeness may be seen in the winged animals of Persian art at Susa. The Persians also borrowed the stone column from Karnak and Luxor in Egypt.

All these great monuments were constructed by slave labor. In the pyramid age the pharaoh fed and housed all the workers. Food and shelter were so important that workmen enslaved themselves. Work on the pyramids took years, and this meant that the workers did not worry about a subsistence as long as they had work. During the period of the New Kingdom, about 1550-1100 B.C., slave workers were captured by the Egyptian army and were put to work on government public works, in the temple workshops and on the estates of the pharaoh and the nobility. Amen-hotep II brought back 90,000 slave laborers from Syria and Palestine, including 3,600 Habiru people related to the Hebrews. This was in 1495-1490 B.C. when the Israelites were being enslaved in Egypt. Tens of thousands of foreigners were slave workers.

The priests used magic charms, incantations, and writings to maintain their power over the people. The Nile Valley with its disease-breeding marshes was not the healthiest place to live. There were periodical plagues of frogs and locusts like those described in the Bible. Even today when the Nile reaches its height in August, the water sometimes becomes red from tiny red organisms which infest it. Hot desert winds blow up thick sand and dust storms. The Egyptians believed demons caused all these catastrophes, even the deaths of so many babies and children. An ancient religious text advised a woman to feed her sick child a mixture of onion, honey, and fish, and defy the demon by saying, "Comst thou to kiss this child? I will not let thee kiss him!"

Perhaps the belief that the dead lived in or at their tombs was the result of the soil and dry Egyptian climate which preserved everything including animal matter. The science of embalming and mumification was developed to make sure the dead were preserved with their hearts. When a man entered the nether world, it was important for him to possess his heart. The Egyptians feared the demons who came from the dead whose bodies had not been preserved and who stole hearts. Scribes wrote long texts from the Book of the Dead on papyrus 16 feet in length, of not permitting a man's heart to be taken away from him in the nether world. These scrolls have been found in tombs by archae-

Courtesy Metropolitan Museum of Art

Two photographs of tomb figures: a weaving shop, and a fishing and fowling skiff.

ologists, along with the lists of a man's good deeds to make him righteous before Osiris:

> "I did not take milk from the mouth of a child.
> I caused no one to weep.
> I did not commit murder."

The ancient Egyptians did not believe in immortality of the soul as we understand it. All the monumental tombs and mortuary furniture were to maintain the deceased in the hereafter without assistance from his surviving relatives. If a man led a righteous life, he was blessed by the sun god, Osiris, who rose in the heavens each morning and descended at night into the netherworld, which was really his home. Every day he was reborn again.

About 1350 B.C. Amenhotep IV, who changed his name to Ikhnaton, conceived the idea of one sun god Aton, a sort of monotheism which was short-lived. John A. Wilson writes that there was no effective transmission of the monotheistic idea between Egypt and the Israelites for these reasons: as slaves on government building projects they had no opportunity for discussion with priests and scribes; the god that the Israelites brought into the land of Canaan was a god of desert simplicity and in no way related to the sophisticated concepts of Amon or Re or Horus; by the time the Israelites were producing literature and seeking models in older forms of literature, Egypt was senile and declining.

Egypt did produce a great literature which the Biblical writers acknowledge in a backhand manner by saying that Solomon's wisdom was greater than that of Egypt and the wisdom of the East. Solomon brought Egyptian scribes to his court to teach writing and with them came some of the lore of Egypt.

Now let us take a look at some of Egypt's literature that may have influenced Israel. Thousands of hymns, poems, stories, proverbs, as well as religious texts have been found written on papyri found in excavations and tombs.

The Egyptian story of creation makes Ptah, the god of Memphis, the first capitol of Egypt, the heart and tongue or the intelligence behind creation. The Egyptians, who were not as a rule abstract thinkers but expressed everything through pictures, had no word for mind, so heart represented mind and tongue, speech. Why was there creation? There was the intelligence of Ptah behind creation. From a translation by Erman, it reads:

"It is the heart which causes every completed concept to come forth, and it is the tongue which announces what the heart thinks. Thus all the gods were formed . . . indeed all the divine order came into being through what the heart thought and the tongue commanded . . . Thus justice was given to him who does what is desired, and punishment to him who does what is not desired. Thus life was given to him who has peace, and death was given to him who has sin. Thus were made all the work and all the crafts, the action of the arms, the movement of the legs, and the activity of every member of the body, in conformance with the command which the heart thought, which came forth through the tongue, and which gives the value of everything. And so it comes to pass that it is said of Ptah, 'He who made everything and brought the gods into being.' . . . So Ptah was satisfied after he had made everything as well as the divine order."

This can be read, "So Ptah rested," and is like Genesis 2:2, "And on the seventh day God finished his work which he had made; and he rested on the seventh day . . ." Breasted writes, "We should not fail to understand in this earliest philosophical religious system, that the world which Ptah brought forth was merely the Egyptian Nile valley." Breasted pointed out that men discerned for the first time in human history that "God gave life to the peaceful and death to the guilty."

The wisdom of Ptah-hotep goes back to the fifth dynasty about 2500 B.C. This was a period when the priests became powerful, and ambitious men climbed the ladder to power and success. The architect Nekhebu tells his success story: "His majesty found me a common builder. His majesty conferred upon me the successive offices of journeyman, master builder, and master of a craft. Next his majesty conferred upon me the successive offices of Royal Constructor and Builder, Royal Attache, and Royal Constructor and Architect . . . His majesty did all this because his majesty favored me so greatly. . . ."

Did Nekhebu climb so high by ability and work? Did he use some of Ptah-hotep's advice on how to succeed in life?

About 1,500 years before Solomon, Ptah-hotep, a wise old man of 110 years who was vizier to the king, asked permission to teach his son so that he would be wise enough to take his father's place as vizier and would be successful in life. Solomon's proverbs had the same purpose. By reading a proverb of Ptah-hotep and then one from the Bible, this is very obvious.

Ptah-hotep: The wise man rises early in the morning to establish himself; but the fool rises early in the morning only to distract himself.

Proverbs, 20:13: Love not sleep lest you come to poverty; open your eyes and you will have plenty of bread.

We all know the ditty of Benjamin Franklin:

"Early to bed and early to rise
Makes a man healthy, wealthy and wise."

Ptah-hotep: A good walker will come to the end of his journey.

Proverbs, 20:7: A righteous man who walks in his integrity—blessed are his sons after him!

Ptah-hotep: Be not avaricious in dividing—be not avaricious toward thy kin. Greater is the fame of the gentle than the harsh.

Proverbs, 21:26: All day long the wicked covets, but the righteous gives and does not hold back. Proverbs, 21:21: He who pursues righteousness and kindness will find life and honor.

Ptah-hotep: It is an ornament of the heart to hear kindly.

Proverbs, 18:13: If one gives answer before he hears it is his folly and shame.

J. H. Breasted, in his book *Development of Religion and Thought in Ancient Egypt,* points out a parallel between a priest under Sen-usert II (1897-1878 B.C.) and Nathan, the prophet under King David.

This was in the Middle Empire, and the empire was disintegrating, to be captured by the Hyksos a century later. The priest places the responsibility for the misery of the people, and corruption, on the king. "Thou art the man. Taste, knowledge, and righteousness are with thee, but it is a strife which thou puttest in the land together with the sound of tumult. Lo, one makes attack upon another. Men conform to what thou hast commanded. If three men go upon the road, they are found to be two, for they who are many slay the few . . . Wherefore thou commandest to make answer: Is it because one man loves, but another hates? Nay, I say thou hast so done as to bring forth these things. Thou hast spoken lies."

Second Samuel, 12:7-9: And Nathan said to David: "Thou art the man. Thus saith the Lord, the God of Israel. I appointed thee king over Israel, and I delivered thee out of the hand of Saul, and I gave thee thy master's house and thy master's wives into thy bosom, and gave thee the house of Israel and of Judah . . . Wherefore hast thou despised the word of the Lord, to do that which is evil in My sight?"

There are also parallels between the hymn of Ikhnaton in the 14th century B.C. and the 104th Psalm in the Bible.

"Thy dawning is beautiful in the horizon of the sky,
O living Aton, Beginning of Life!
When thou risest in the eastern horizon,
Thou fillest every land with beauty.
Thou art beautiful, great, glittering, high above land.
Thy rays, they encompass the lands, even all that
thou hast made.
Thou art Re, and thou carriest them all away captive.
Thou bindest them by thy love.
Though thou art far away, thy rays are upon earth;
Though thou art on high, thy footprints are the day."

The 104th Psalm: 1-5
"O Lord my God, Thou art very great;
Thou art clothed with glory and majesty.
Who coverest Thyself with light as a garment,
Who stretchest out the heavens like a curtain;
Who layest the beams of Thine upper chambers in the
waters,
Who makest the clouds Thy chariot,
Who walkest upon the wings of the wind;
Who makest winds Thy messengers,
The flaming fire Thy ministers."

From the late empire, after the invasions of new people from the sea, come the love songs, rejoicing in nature and the open air. The word for sweetheart in both cultures is "sister."

The Egyptian poet sings:

"Would that thou wouldst come to the sister speedily,
Like a horse of the King
Picked from a thousand of all steeds,
The foremost of the stables . . .
When it hears the sound of the whip,
It knows no delay,
And there is no chief charioteer
Who can stand before it.
How well the sister's heart knows
That he is not far from the sister."
In the Song of Songs, Chapter 1:9:
"I have compared thee O my love,
To a steed in Pharaoh's chariots."

Egyptian civilization had an originality that has remained unique to this day. Pyramids, mummies, obelisks are peculiarly Egyptian. The beautiful form of her art styles and hieroglyphs have never been surpassed.

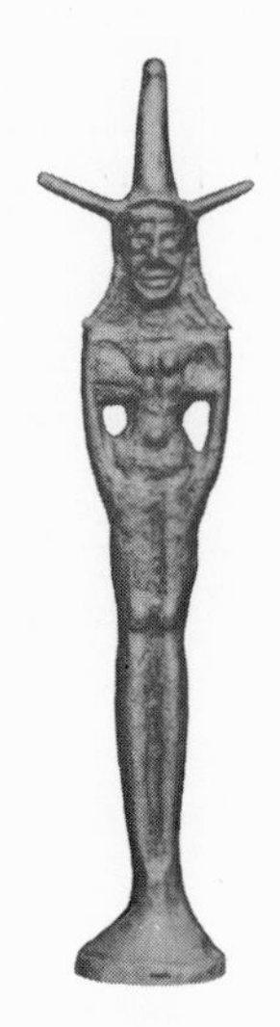

CHAPTER VII

THE DESERT IS SPREAD THROUGHOUT THE LAND

"Sargon the mighty King, king of Agade am I."

THUS BEGINS THE romantic poem about Sargon I (ca. 2360) who founded the first empire by conquest. From a tablet found at Nippur, we learn that "Sargon, King of Agade was victorious in a battle with the inhabitants of Ur. . . ." Further on, ". . . Sargon, King of Kish was victorious in 34 campaigns and dismantled all the cities as far as the shore of the sea. . . . Sargon the king prostrated himself before the god Dagon in Tutul, and he gave him the upper region of Mari . . . as far as the Cedar Forest and the Silver Mountain." This means Sargon conquered the cedar forests of Lebanon and the mountains of silver and lapis lazuli in Asia Minor, extending his empire from the Caspian Sea to the Persian Gulf and controlling raw materials which were not found in Mesopotamia. Into the conquered towns were introduced temple corporations dedicated to Ishtar, cuneiform writing, industry, and trade.

The Old Kingdom of Egypt had her trading port at Byblos where her ships were loaded with the cedar wood so necessary for tombs, boats, and furniture. There the Egyptians shipped copper from the mines in Sinai to the Mediterranean islands and traded in wine, silver, lapis lazuli, and obsidian.

In the sixth dynasty, about 2300 B.C., the Egyptian temple at Byblos burned down, and trade ended over the caravan road through Palestine. This precipitated the end of the Old Kingdom which had been disintegrating for a long time.

An Egyptian sage described the general distress of his country: "The doorkeepers say, let us go plunder. The washerman refuseth to carry his load. The bird catchers have made themselves ready for battle, and others from the Delta carry shields. Even the most peaceful callings such as confectioners and brewers are in revolt, and a man looketh upon his son as an enemy . . . the virtuous man goeth in mourning because of what hath happened in the land . . . strangers are becoming Egyptians everywhere."

This gives us another clue as to why the Old Kingdom collapsed, besides loss of trade. The people refused to continue as slave laborers dedicated to building tombs. The country was torn with civil war until about 2000 B.C. and the rise of the Middle Kingdom at Thebes.

Who were these people in the Delta carrying shields?

They were a horde of Semitic tribes from the Arabian desert known as Amorites and Aramaeans. They overran Mesopotamia and toppled the empires built up by Sargon I and his successor, Naram-Sin. The Amorites took over the Akkadian Empire, and it became Babylonia. Other Amorites caused distress in the Syrian cities of Ugarit and Byblos and then invaded Palestine where they destroyed city after city, and some of them settled in the hill country of Palestine. They destroyed towns but did not rebuild them because they were tent dwellers who truly made the desert triumphant over the sown. Their dead were housed in rock-cut tombs. In those Amorite tombs that have been excavated, javelins made of copper have been found beside the skeletons. Javelins were the new weapon of this period. The Egyptians did not have them, and this may be one reason they could not hold back the invaders.

From 2000 B.C. on through the second millennium migrating peoples converged on the areas of the Mediterranean, southwestern and southeastern Asia, and the Nile valley.

They came in waves from the plains of the Caucasus, eastern Europe, northern Mesopotamia, the Arabian desert, Nubia, Libya and, like tidal waves, enveloped, destroyed, settled, or pushed on, leaving behind desolation.

Why did they migrate to the Fertile Crescent? No doubt the

basic causes were crop failures and resulting famines. They may have been driven from their homes by epidemics, earthquakes, floods, forest fires, wars in which invaders ousted them from their homes. The advanced civilizations of the Fertile Crescent offered many enticements: warm climates, abundant food, substantial mud brick shelters, the mystery of gods and temples, the splendor of the kings, the booty from plunder of gold and silver, jewels, clothing, weapons, slaves, and tribute from conquered nations.

At the beginning of the second millennium the Hittites, an Indo-European people, came down from the high Taurus mountains to the interior highlands and coasts of Asia Minor, the site of modern Turkey. They superimposed their Indo-European Hittite language on the country which was known as Hatti, and about 1600 B.C. were known as the Early Hittite Empire.

Kassite hordes from the eastern plateaus of Asia overthrew the dynasty of Hammurabi about 1600 B.C. Around this time the Mycenaeans from the Greek mainland took over the Minoan culture on the island of Crete.

Another Indo-European people, who came from the country north of the Caspian and Black seas, the Vedic Aryans, established themselves on the upper Euphrates at Mitanni, in Persia, and in India from about 1500 to 1200 B.C. These people were nomadic, hut-dwelling people who brought with them the horse, armor, butter, hearth and fire worship.

By 1200 B.C. iron-sworded Dorians from Europe fought their way south to Greece and wrecked Aegean civilizations, sending swarms of sea people from the Greek islands into Palestine, Syria and Egypt.

These invasions caused dark ages, and few buildings and inscriptions survive for the archaeological record. As we approach the early second millennium when the patriarch Abraham lived, there is a possibility, according to G. Ernest Wright, "that the patriarchal clans were involved in the 'barbarian' invasions which brought to a temporary halt the flourishing cultures of the Near East about 2000 B.C." Some of these "barbarians," the invading Amorites, settled on the Middle Euphrates and built the kingdom of Mari. In 1933 Andre Parrot from the Musée du Louvre found that Mari was one of the most prosperous cities in Mesopotamia. The last king Zimri-lim carried on a correspondence with Hammurabi King of Babylon. This correspondence was found among 20,000 clay tablets in the archives of the palace, which was a tremendous structure covering more than fifteen acres. Besides the royal apartments it contained administrative offices and a school for scribes. Portions of mural paintings show scenes of sacrifice with the king of Mari receiving from Ishtar the staff and ring of his authority. A ziggurat and temple were dedicated to Ishtar. Mari fell to Hammurabi in the thirty-second year of the reign of Zimri-Lim.

In the archives of Mari was found a letter to Zimri-Lim mentioning the issue of clothing by an enemy king to Habiru soldiers. Another tablet mentions thirty Habiru who have come from a district north of Babylonia. In other texts these Habiru are described as foreigners, but are not considered nomads since they have a permanent home. The name Habiru has been identified with Hebrew, in connection with Abraham who is called "the Hebrew" (Gen. 14:13). Habiru did not refer to a particular race, but rather to the status of a foreigner.

Other striking evidence for the origin of the Patriarchs in northern Mesopotamia comes from Nuzi, a town southwest of Nineveh which was settled by the Hurrians. They were an Armenoid people who overran Syria and Palestine, and pushed into north Mesopotamia as early as 2000 B.C. They were called Horites in the Bible (Gen. 14:6). Hurrian scribes wrote in the Babylonian language sometimes using Hurrian words. Thousands of these clay tablets were found by the American School of Oriental Research at Bagdad from 1927-31. Many of the customs and laws of the Hurrians at Nuzi cast light on the incidents of the Biblical Patriarchs. Let us follow the wanderings of Abraham in the Book of Genesis from Ur to Canaan.

CHAPTER VIII

ABRAHAM, FATHER OF A FAITH

When Abraham entered the historical scene about 1950 B.C. order had been restored to his native city of Ur and the Kings of Larsa ruled. Ur-Nammu established a law code which was discussed in Chapter V. With the dissolution of Sargon's empire, the country was once more ruled by city states, which were continually fighting each other.

Abraham's father Terah bought and sold cattle. No doubt he pastured his herds outside the city and lived a semi-nomadic life. Let us assume he lived in a house during his residence in Ur. According to Leonard Wooley's excavations of Ur, the house was built of whitewashed mud brick on a narrow, crowded street. Merchants sat in spaces between the houses and sold bread, fruit, pottery, woolen cloth, copper ornaments. Up the street was a school where Abraham, along with other students, was taught to write on a wet clay tablet with a stylus. Excavators found over 2000 clay tablets in the ruins of this school. In cuneiform wedge-shaped writing were copies of religious texts and inscriptions on monuments, practice exercises in arithmetic. According to these tablets Abraham could have been familiar with multiplication and division tables, square and cube root. Some of the ancient school boys did exercises in practical mathematics by trying to find the exact measurements of an odd-shaped field.

The excavators found that in the time of Abraham it was the custom to bury the dead under the floor of the courtyard of each house. Above this courtyard was a family chapel with an offering table on which were little terra cotta figures, small cups and plates for food offerings. Incense was burned in a fireplace which also heated the upper part of the house. Woolley observed that the altars in some houses were made of unhewn stone and placed on burnt earth that had been purified. He surmised that these altars of unhewn stone might have belonged to the people of the Habiru tribes, for it was a rule among the Israelites to build their altars of unhewn stone. Exodus 20:25, "And if thou wilt make me an altar of unhewn stone, thou shalt not build it of hewn stone, for if thou lift up thy tool upon it thou hast polluted it."

Perhaps the legend of Abraham breaking all his father's idols but one, took place at this shrine. He put a tiny stick in the hand of the remaining idol. When his father scolded him he said, "The idol with the stick broke all the others."

His father said, "An idol can't do that."

Abraham asked, "Why do we pray to them? Isn't there one god we cannot see who rules the world?"

This is just a legend. Abraham prayed to one god. That god may have been his family god, because Abraham's father worshipped other gods. Joshua 24:2, "Your father dwelt of old time beyond the river, even Terah and the father of Nahor; and they served other gods."

Abraham grew to manhood in Ur and there married Sarah. They had no children. His brother Nahor died, and left a son, Lot. Then Terah decided to move the family to Haran where many of his kinsmen had settled.

Abraham in Haran

Haran still exists as a town on the Balikh River in northwest Mesopotamia. Cuneiform tablets show it was a prosperous city in the nineteenth and eighteenth centuries B.C. The city of Nahor, which has the same name as Abraham's brother, was the home of Rebekah and is mentioned in the Mari tablets as Nakhur. Other towns in the vicinity bear the names of Abraham's ancestors mentioned in Genesis 11:22-27. Serugi is named for a great-grandfather, Serug; Philiga for a remote ancestor, Peleg; Til-Turakhi for Terah.

While his father Terah lived, Abraham lived in Haran. After

Terah's death, the Lord said to Abraham (Gen. 12:1-2), "Get thee out of thy country, and from thy kindred, and from thy father's house, unto a land I will show thee. And I will make thee a great nation, and I will bless thee and make thy name great." So Abraham took his wife Sarah, his nephew Lot, and members of his clan, and began the long trek south.

Abraham in the Negev

Abraham's route, according to a map by Nelson Glueck, was west to Carchemish, south to Aleppo, Hamath, Damascus, and Shechem, which was in the land of Canaan. There he built an altar, and the Lord appeared to Abraham and said (Genesis 12:7), "Unto thy seed will I give this land." On a mountain east of Bethel he built another altar and pitched his tents.

As he wandered south, Abraham began to understand why the Canaanites sacrificed their first-born to Baal, the rain god. The hills were parched yellow from no rain. There was a drought. Crops failed. Cattle were dying. Perhaps a sacrifice to Baal might bring rain.

At this time Palestine was unsettled. During the invasions many of the farmers had fled, and the land lay fallow. The invaders were nomads who did not produce food. There was a famine in Canaan. Abraham pushed south, to Hebron, Beersheba, across Sinai into Egypt.

The kings of the twelfth dynasty of the Middle Kingdom were good rulers. They built a huge catch basin at Faiyum for the fast-moving waters of the Nile inundation, and opened up a large area for cultivation. There was plenty of food in Egypt, and the country was prosperous. Hungry people from drought-stricken lands like Palestine flocked into Egypt. The tomb painting of a powerful noble, Khumhotep at Beni Hasan, near Cairo, in the reign of Sen-usert II, fourth king of the twelfth dynasty, shows us what Abraham and his clan might have looked like. Thirty-seven Asiatics from the desert come bringing gifts and desiring trade. The men have pointed beards and their thick black hair is neck-length. Both men and women wear woolen tunics made by sewing brightly colored strips together. Those of the men are knee-length, the women's reach to the middle of their legs. Some of the men wear long white tunics, the others wear white ones to the knee. The men wear sandals while the women wear low leather boots. There is a child in just a knee-length skirt. Their weapons consist of a composite bow, which is built up of wood, sinew, and horn glued together and can be shot at a long distance and penetrate the victim. They also had throw sticks and darts. One of the men carried a lyre and part of the load carried by one of the asses were bellows, which showed they were metal workers.

Abraham returned to Caanan from Egypt very rich in cattle, silver, and gold. He did not stay, for in Egypt the king was God. Everybody and everything was the property of the king. Abraham returned to Palestine. At Sodom by the Dead Sea where Lot had settled, some kings of small cities were revolting. The earth was scorched and destroyed from the wars by the overlord Chedorlaomer, who was aided by Amraphel of Shinar and two other kings. Lot was captured. Abraham, now the chief of three hundred fighting men, rescued Lot. This won the respect of all the chieftains in the Negev, including the king of Salem. Nobody molested Abraham when he chose to settle at Hebron.

The Egyptian story of Sinuhe, who lived in Palestine and prospered during this period, gives us an idea of how Abraham lived. Sinuhe described the land: "There were figs in it, and vines, and it had more wine than water. Plentiful was its honey, abundant its olives. Every kind of fruit was on its trees. Barley was there and emmer. There was no limit to any kind of cattle."

The trade routes were open to Syria and Mesopotamia, and Sinuhe led expeditions against marauding Bedouins. He also entertained visitors from Egypt. His door was open to the traveler. He gave water to the thirsty, set him upon the road that had strayed, rescued him that had been plundered. Later, Sinuhe was pardoned and returned to Egypt.

Nelson Glueck discovered a chain of settlements along the ancient trade routes of the Negev from the time of Abraham. Foundations show the houses to be made of stone and oval-shaped.

From the clay tablets discovered at Nuzi, we know that Abraham was a civilized man and lived by Mesopotamian law. This explains some of the stories in Genesis. According to the law of Nuzi, a childless wife must provide her husband with a handmaiden to bear him children, and the offspring cannot be driven away. This is why Sarah provided Abraham with Hagar, and why he was fearful to cast her out with Ishmael.

It was another custom for childless couples to adopt a son who would look after them in their old age and eventually inherit their property. Such a person was Eliezer of Damascus, whom Abraham described as one who would possess his house, when he complained to God he was childless (Genesis 15:2). After the birth of Isaac, Eliezer was no longer Abraham's heir.

Life was hard in that arid country. When his barley fields began to wither and his lambs and kids died of thirst, Abraham began to wonder if sacrificing his son Isaac to God would cause rain to fall. He thought he heard the voice of God telling him to sacrifice Isaac. He went up to a high place and built an altar, and placed his son upon it. Just as he was about to kill the boy he heard a noise. It was a ram caught in some bushes. There is a Mesopotamian saying,

> The lamb is the substitute for humanity;
> He hath given up a lamb for his life.

Abraham sacrificed the lamb in place of Isaac.

Child sacrifice was one of the hideous parts of the Canaanite religion. As late as the seventh century B.C. in the reign of Israel's backsliding King Manasseh, followers of the Canaanite religion sacrificed children. II Chronicles 33:6, "He also made his children to pass through the fire. . ." The story of the sacrifice of Isaac was written in the eighth century B.C. by the great Biblical writers to teach that God demands obedience from man, but not the sacrifice of his first-born. An animal was provided as a substitute. The medieval philosopher Maimonides saw Abraham as a thinking man, who grasped the fact that idolatry is foolish and illogical. His mind was filled with the knowledge and love of God, and what he held in himself he tried to give to others.

Biblical archaeology helps us see Abraham as a man, an historical figure, in a period of confusion.

CHAPTER IX

THE HYKSOS IN EGYPT AND PALESTINE

BY THE EIGHTEENTH CENTURY B.C. the migratory hordes from the north and northeast had gradually moved south into the Fertile Crescent. Palestine and Syria were already occupied by strange people who were rebelling against Egypt. The Egyptians called these people Hyksos, or Shepherd Kings.

In 1926 the Berlin Museum published texts written on broken pieces of pottery bowls found at Thebes. Shortly after, texts similar to those written on the sherds of bowls were found written on fragments of clay figurines. These writings on pottery were curses on the enemies of the Pharaoh and are known as the execration texts. This ceremony went back to the Old Kingdom. In the Pyramid texts it was called "breaking the red jars."

The Pharaoh was seated on his throne, as slaves brought in red pottery jars, covered with writing and figurines covered with writing. The grand vizier took a jar from a slave and read: "All men, all people, all folk, all males, all eunuchs, all females, and all nobles, who may plot, who may fight, who may think of fighting, or who may think of rebelling, and every rebel who thinks of rebelling—in this entire land!"

Then the Grand Vizier gave the pot to Pharaoh, who stood up and threw the pot to the floor where it broke in pieces, as he shouted, "Cursed be them all!"

One after the other the Pharaoh smashed pots and figurines

Courtesy Brussels Museum

Clay figurine of a bound prisoner inscribed with a curse and broken to make the curse effective.

after the execration texts were read. Some of them he condemned to death, shouting, "Sen Usert, daughter of Sit-Ameni, shall die!"

As each bowl or figurine smashed on the floor it was supposed to create a magic spell that would bring harm to the enemies of the Pharaoh.

Cursing enemies and smashing bowls might have been an emotional outlet for the rulers of Egypt, but it did not keep the government from disintegrating, or the defenses from collapsing. The Egyptian army crumbled before the Hyksos who wore body armor, and rode in chariots pulled by fast horses. They had superior weapons: bronze tipped arrows and strong bronze swords and daggers. They introduced the composite bow into warfare. It was built up of layers of wood, sinew and horn glued together. This bow had far greater striking distance and penetration than the simple little bows of the Egyptian forces.

The Hyksos entrenched themselves at Avaris-Tanis in the Delta. Their camp still stands at modern Tel el-Yahudiyeh and is a great plaster faced sandbank. In Hyksos times it was a huge rectangular enclosure of beaten earth, 400 yards long on a side with an embankment from 15 to 20 yards high.

The Hyksos allowed the Pharaoh to live at Thebes and did not bother with him as long as he paid his tribute. These people were not barbarians. They were a mixture of Semites and Indo-European Hurrians. What caused their great migration southward is not known, unless other migrating peoples drove them out of their homeland. The greatest migration of the Hyksos took place in the early seventeenth century B.C. Excavations in Palestine show that during this period towns were destroyed and rebuilt several times. As soon as the Hyksos conquered a town they fortified it with rectangular walls whose sloping embankments were plastered on the outside. Excavations at Jericho revealed a street of cobbled steps by which the people climbed the bank to enter the town. Beneath the steps were well-built drains. Some of these fortresses, like those excavated at Megiddo and Shechem, were entered by means of a ramp, and the gateway flanked by towers was wide enough for two horse-driven chariots to enter at one time. The largest Hyksos fortress was excavated by Yigael Yadin at Hazor in north Galilee. This massive bank was a thousand yards long, and 500 yards wide. Here the Hyksos kept many horses and chariots.

Palestine was sparsely populated before this period, but the Hyksos brought in skilled people and established fortified towns, particularly in the Judean hills. They destroyed many old towns like Khirbet Kerak south of the Sea of Galilee where a fine red and black burnished ware had been made. The Hyksos introduced a fast pottery wheel which turned out jars with pointed bases and loop handles, bowls with sharply angular forms, and dipper juglets with a single handle and pinched mouth. This new pottery was covered over with a deep red slip and given a highly burnished finish. Some of the pots were often finished on the wheel with very fine combing. The red burnished pottery with angular forms are like some silver bowls found in Byblos. These pottery bowls gave the illusion of metal by smearing thick coats of red or cream slip after the clay had dried leather-hard. Then they were burnished with stone or bone until they shone like copper or silver. An independent high art was developed at this time in beautifully carved metal work. Toggle pins made of metal were used for holding garments together.

It is possible the Hyksos brought in the vertical loom and the weaving of woolen cloth, which developed into a big industry in Palestine. They dyed their cloth rich shades of red or blue, preparing the dye from a shellfish called the murex. This was an important industry in Phoenicia, and piles of murex shells have been found at Byblos and other Syrian coast cities. Great quantities of clay loom weights were found in a house of the Middle Bronze period at Jericho.

In the seventeenth century B.C. Palestine was the center of a Northwest Semitic empire ruled from the northeastern corner of the Nile Delta. During the reign of the Hyksos kings, Apophis and Ka-mose, Palestine was the highroad of trade between Africa and Asia. Many of the Hyksos nobility and patricians were Hurrians. These chieftains lived in strongly fortified settlements in Palestine, and were constantly fighting each other. A palace of one of the nobility was excavated at Tell Beit Mirsim in the low hill country southwest of Hebron. It may have been first built in the seventeenth century, was completely destroyed and rebuilt just before the Egyptians expelled the Hyksos in 1550 B.C. Similar large mansions were found at Megiddo, Bethel, Shechem, Jericho, and elsewhere. The largest palace was at Tell el-Ajjul situated at the Palestine end of the desert road leading into the Hyksos capital at Avaris. This strongly fortified house was built around a court opening into rows and rows of rooms. Living quarters for the master were on the second floor. A tomb at Jericho shows us that their burial practices were similar to those of Egypt. It contained an entire family—adults, adolescents, and children. There were pottery jars for water, and plates to eat a roasted sheep that had also been buried. The dead lay on rush mats; in the center of the group a man lay on a bed. Like the Egyptians, the dead were supplied with furniture. A narrow three-legged table and stools were in the tomb to make their life in the nether-world comfortable. On the shoulders of the skeletons were the toggle pins that fastened their garments together. All had a scarab either on a bronze finger ring or suspended around the neck. Carved wooden combs lay by some of the heads, and some fragments of braided hair were found. Each adult had supplies of toilet articles, like a juglet for oil, a basket holding little wooden boxes decorated with bone carvings, an extra supply of combs, an alabaster juglet for oil and scent, and in some cases a wig. All this was so well preserved that the reconstruction of a room in Jericho of this period is completely factual. Only fragments of textiles were not preserved. It is surmised an epidemic must have caused the death of this entire family.

In contrast to the palaces of the nobility are remains of hovels of the lower class who were half-free serfs and lived wretchedly.

At last in 1550 B.C. the Hyksos were expelled from Egypt into Palestine. For three years the Hyksos princes of Palestine resisted the Egyptian and Nubian armies at Sharuhen (Tell el Farah, at the edge of the southern desert).

Following the Hyksos regime all the land in Egypt belonged to the Pharaoh. This is regarded as a clue that Joseph lived in Egypt during the rule of the Hyksos. (Gen. 47:20-22), "So Joseph bought all the land of Egypt for Pharaoh; for all the Egyptians sold their fields, because the famine was severe upon them. The land became Pharaoh's, and as for the people he made slaves of them from one end of Egypt to the other. Only the land of the priests he did not buy."

The length of the time the Israelites lived in Egypt according to Exodus 12:40 was 430 years. According to Numbers 13:22, "Hebron was built seven years before Zo'an in Egypt." Zo'an was the same as Avaris Tanis, the Hyksos capitol.

There is an Egyptian stele that celebrates the founding of Avaris-Tanis, and does honor to the god Seth dressed as an Asiatic. This stele is dated 1330 or 1325 B.C. and marked the beginning of the god Seth at Avaris Tanis around 1725 B.C. or 1730 B.C. There are 400 years between the dates. The Exodus took place in the early thirteenth century B.C. So we can calculate that Joseph and his brothers were in Egypt at the time of the Hyksos.

It is impossible to date the sojourn in Egypt. Egyptian records do not show that the Israelites or Habiru were captured and enslaved.

From Egyptian literature comes a story similar to the Biblical story of Joseph's temptation by Potiphar's wife, and is called "The

Tale of the Two Brothers." A younger brother was tempted by his sister-in-law, and he repulsed her. The scorned woman claimed she was outraged and caused him much misfortune. This story was found on a papyrus dated about 1209-1205 B.C. in the reign of Seti II. No doubt there was a Joseph for when a man is a hero all sorts of similar stories grow up about him.

After the expulsion of the Hyksos, Thutmose III was the great conqueror of the New Empire whose kingdom extended from the Greek islands on the west, to the fourth cataract of the Nile in the south, and in the north included Palestine, Syria, the coasts of Asia Minor and the highlands of the Upper Euphrates. The victory of Thutmose III caused a poet to write a hymn to a new god. "He seeth the whole world hourly." No longer was Egypt's horizon fixed by the fringes of the Nile. She had come out of her isolation. The dominion of the Sun God was universal—the whole world—all men! The thinking men of Egypt conceived a monotheistic religion! Was this not confirmed by Egyptian merchants and envoys who had seen the Sun God shine upon the ziggurats of Babylonia, the kingdom of the Hittites, the islands of Greece? Inscribed on a stele of stone in the British Museum is the Sun hymn written by two twin brothers, Suti and Hor, architects for Amenhotep III who was building temples and palaces at Thebes.

"Hail to thee, beautiful god of every day!
Sole Lord, taking captive all lands every day,
As one beholding them that walk therein."

Amenhotep IV dedicated himself to the new sun god Aton—changed his name to Ikhnaton and built a new capitol at Amarna. The graceful bas-reliefs of himself and his beautiful sister wife Nefert-iti can be seen on a stele which shows them worshipping the sundisk.

During Ikhnaton's preoccupation with religion his governors in Syria and Palestine sent letters written in cuneiform on clay tablets asking for help against raiders. These are the Amarna Letters. Abdi-Khepa, governor of Jerusalem, wrote: "The Habiru plunder all the land of the king." Or, "The Habiru are taking the cities of the king." These letters date between 1369 and 1353 B.C. The Habiru might have been those Israelite tribes who did not go to Egypt.

CHAPTER X

THE EXODUS

THERE IS NO archaeological evidence of the Exodus of the Israelites out of Egypt. All scholars agree that this was such an important event in Hebrew history and in the foundation of the Jewish religion, that Biblical history must be accepted.

No archaeological evidence of the Exodus exists because the Israelites were wandering tribes at that time and built no permanent settlements. They lived in tents, their containers were of skin. Even the first Tabernacle was a tent.

There is evidence that not all the tribes who later united into a monarchy under Solomon took part in the Exodus. Some remained in Canaan. In the last chapter, the Amarna letters told of raiding Habiru tribes in Palestine. Leonard Woolley excavating in Turkish Hatay in 1939 found an inscription in a palace of a Hittite King Idri-mi, who found refuge from invaders with a Habiru tribe in the extreme north of Canaan. In later times this territory belonged to the tribes of Asher and Zebulon. The king tells us in the inscription, "I abode among the Habiru warriors for seven years."

Many centuries later, under the monarchy, the celebration of Passover became such an important part of the Jewish religion that all the tribes believed their ancestors took part in it.

There is a possibility that nomad Habiru tribes in southern Palestine joined the Egyptian refugees after they arrived in Sinai. The stiff-necked Israelites whom Moses found unmanageable must have been the nomadic warriors who lived from their herds, used milk as food, and settled temporarily to grow a crop of barley. Nelson Glueck describes finding a hidden valley in the Negev, with a ploughed field of barley ready for harvest, and no sign of human habitation. He surmised some Bedouins had planted the barley in the spring, departed for greener pastures, and intended to harvest it in the fall. So grain did grow in the river bottoms or wadis in the Negev. Nomads are very independent and individualistic. They are very proud and tend to look down on settled people. Evidently these nomadic traits did not leave the Israelites who had settled in Egypt and been enslaved. Egyptian inscriptions show that Bedouins from Palestine and Sinai entered Egypt, "Who knew not how they should live, have come begging for a home in the domain of the Pharaoh."

The route of the Exodus, according to G. Ernest Wright, was about thirty-two miles south of the well-guarded military road to Canaan from Goshen across the Sinai peninsula. They crossed a "Reed Sea," in other words, some marshlands. Wright accounts for this by a mistaken translation of "Yam Suph" as Red Sea, instead of Reed Sea or Marsh Sea. They took this route to get past the string of fortresses with which the Pharaoh guarded the frontier.

In our modern world the Exodus has become a symbol of emancipation for all oppressed peoples. Moses, the great founder of Israel's religion, organized a loosely related group of tribes into a people, with a covenant with God. This covenant was a code of moral laws they must obey if they were to be God's people. Those laws were written on stone, the Ten Commandments which Moses brought down from Mt. Sinai. The God of Mt. Sinai was a jealous God who demanded they worship Him alone. He was their God and they were His people. This made the religion of Israel different from all ancient religions, for God required a man to lead a good life, and to worship one God. This may be contrasted with Aton, the sole Sun God of Ikhnaton, who made no moral demands upon the worshippers. Here began Israel's great contribution to our civilization in the requirement that men lead a moral life to have a good life, and there is but one God whose powers have no limits.

From the desert religion of Exodus developed the great

spiritual religion of the prophets and the writing of the Bible in later centuries.

Moses organized a priesthood which was hereditary, and built a place of worship, a tabernacle which was a tent. In the tent was a wooden box which held the stone tablets on which was written the law. This box was called the Ark. It was carried about on long poles.

The Arabs, before the time of Mohammed, possessed sacred tents which were carried from place to place on the backs of camels. Such a tent-shrine is on a bas-relief from the temple of Bel at Palmyra during the Roman period.

After the settlement of Palestine the religion of Israel centered about this Ark. God's goodness and power by delivering them from Egypt, giving the laws and requiring by a covenant that they obey those laws and worship but one God, bound the tribes into a people.

In the time of the Patriarchs, the tribes worshipped the God of Abraham, Isaac, and Jacob. God had revealed his name as Yahweh to Moses in the desert by means of a burning bush that did not burn. The God who had revealed himself to Moses demanded a much higher standard of behavior than did other Semitic religions. Thus Judaism began in the desert.

The first mention of Israel in any Egyptian text comes in 1230 B.C. when the Sea People attempted to invade Egypt and the Pharaoh Mer-ne-Ptah defeated them. This poem celebrates his victory:

> "The princes are prostrate saying, 'Mercy!'
> Not one raises his head among the Nine Bows.
> Desolation is for Tehenu. Hatti is pacified.
> Plundered is the Canaan with every evil;
> Carried off is Ashkelon; seized upon is Gezer;
> Yanoam is made as that which does not exist;
> Israel is laid waste, his seed is not;
> Palestine is become a widow for Egypt!"

This verse has no historical meaning for us except that Egypt recognized a people known as Israel somewhere in Palestine or Transjordan.

CHAPTER XI
THE CONQUEST OF CANAAN

ABOUT 1240 B.C., after the exodus from Egypt, the Israelites, a group of loosely allied tribes, entered Canaan under the leadership of Joshua. They worshipped their national god Yahweh. He was their god, and they were His people.

After the Egyptians had expelled the Hyksos, they conquered Palestine where they were brutally and cruelly oppressive. Archaeologists have found stelae and statues in Palestine. A famous stele of Sethos I found in the garrison city of Beth-shan dated around 1318 B.C. tells of a treaty with the Hittites. Most of the Egyptian activity took place in the coastal regions. Sinai and the Negev possessed no strongly fortified towns like those in the north, but was a wilderness where nomadic tribes pitched their tents and grazed their flocks wherever they pleased. These desert tribes were friendly to the Israelites. Otherwise the conquest would not have been possible.

Moses had sent Joshua and Caleb to lead a party of men to spy out the land. After forty days of reconnaissance they returned with grapes, figs, and pomegranates and said, "The land to which you sent us is one of milk and honey and this is the fruit to prove it. The towns are walled and heavily fortified. We won't be able to conquer these people."

Archaeological excavations of the fortified Canaanite towns show the spies to be right. It was impossible to enter Canaan from the south over the caravan road between Mesopotamia and Egypt.

The people refused to listen to the spies, but insisted on marching north. They were attacked by the Amalkekites and the Canaanites and badly defeated at Hormah.

The reoccupation by the Israelites was very slow. They were not able to break through the chariots and fortifications of the Canaanites.

The conquest was really guerrilla warfare, for the Israelites were not equipped to lay siege to a well-fortified city. They fought on foot, with some swords and spears. Bows, slings, staves, and stones were their main weapons. They used the tactic of surprise. Joshua seems to have been a master at outwitting the enemy.

With Egypt controlling the main roads to the north and west, their only hope of entry was from the east, and according to the Bible the first great victory was the Fall of Jericho.

The next city, Bethel-Ai, was taken by the strategy of hiding most of the men a short distance from the city. Joshua with a small force attacked the city, and the King of Ai came out of the city to drive them away. Joshua pretended to retreat but led the enemy right into an ambush, where they were defeated. The city was burned to the ground. Excavations by William Albright show that Bethel-Ai between the fourteenth and early thirteenth century was a flourishing Late Bronze Age city with very well built homes. The city was burnt down, leaving a deposit of as much as a metre and a half of debris. According to Albright the Israelites caused this destruction.

One of the most interesting excavations of the conquest was that of Gibeon conducted by James B. Pritchard during four summers from 1956 to 1960.

The village known as El Jib is located in Jordan. In 1838 Edward Robinson listed El Jib as ancient Gibeon. His theory that Biblical names were faithfully carried down in Arabic names proved to be correct. El Jib was Gibeon.

Pritchard began excavating the saddle-like hill with two clues: 1. That El Jib might be the Arabic name of Gibeon; 2. That it contained broken pottery from jars used in the seventh century B.C. They began excavation on the eastern side of the hill, and found a tunnel with steps down to a spring inside the city wall. They discovered a cylindrical pool hewn from the rock, measuring 37 feet in diameter and 35 feet deep. Going down into the pool was a curved staircase cut into the rock wall. This pool was built sometime between the twelfth and eleventh centuries. The excavators dug out tons of dirt and stone from the pool, and found pottery, pins for clothing, cosmetic instruments used by women to paint their faces, tools, weapons, and most important, some jar handles with writing in Hebrew script which said GB"N —GDR or Gibeon. Now there was no doubt that El Jib was the site of ancient Gibeon. Twenty-four more jar handles inscribed with the name of Gibeon were found in the same rock-cut pool during the course of the excavations, and removed all possibility that the jars were imported from another place. Further excavations disclosed wine cellars with storage jars. No doubt the inscribed handles belonged to wine jars.

Gibeon was a prosperous city, surrounded by massive fortifications and was one of the main wine-producing centers in ancient Israel.

Joshua 10:2 tells us Gibeon was a great city, "Like one of the royal cities . . . and all its men were mighty." In Chapter 9 of Joshua we read that:

When the people of Gibeon heard how Joshua had conquered Jericho and Ai, they acted with cunning. They dressed up in ragged clothing and worn-out shoes, and put old sacks upon their donkeys, and old mended wineskins. Even their provisions of bread were dry and moldy. They went to Joshua's camp in Gilgal and said, "We come from a far country. Will you make a treaty with us?"

The men of Israel answered: "How do we know you do not live here? How can we make a treaty with you?"

"We are your servants," replied the strangers (Joshua 9:1-27).

Joshua insisted, "Who are you?"

"From a far country we have come because of the name of the Lord your God; for we have heard a report of him and all that he did in Egypt." They had heard of all the conquests of the Israelities and wanted to make a treaty.

Joshua made a treaty with them. Three days later he learned these men had come from Gibeon and were neighbors. He did not attack them because he had made a treaty and would not break his word. He said, "Why did you deceive me, and tell me you come from a far country when you are neighbors? I won't attack you. You shall live." He cursed them saying, "None of you shall be freed from being bondmen, and hewers of wood, and drawers of water. . . ."

When the King of Jerusalem heard of the treaty between Gibeon and Joshua, he and four Amorite kings attacked Gibeon. Now the men of Gibeon without disguises appealed to Joshua for help.

Joshua and his men marched all night from Gilgal and not only defeated the King of Jerusalem and the four Amorite kings at Gilgal but chased them as far as Azekah. The battle was not yet over, and it was getting dark, and Joshua spoke to the Lord, in the day when the Lord delivered up the Amorites to the men of Israel. And he said in the sight of Israel: (Joshua 10:12, 14).

> "Sun, stand thou still at Gibeon,
> and thou Moon in the valley of Aijalon."

The sun stood still and the moon did not come up until the Amorites were beaten. "There has been no day like it before or since, when the Lord hearkened to the voice of a man; for the Lord fought for Israel" (Joshua 10:12, 14).

Pritchard writes it is possible the Sun-god was worshipped at Gibeon and the Moon-god worshipped at Aijalon. The allusion to the religion of the Gibeonites is from the lost Book of Jashar, as indicated by the question in the Bible, "Is this not written in the book of Jashar?"

Excavations reveal violent destruction at Lachish about 1220 B.C. and at Hazor approximately the same time. No doubt these cities must have fallen to Israel.

According to G. Ernest Wright, there were Hebrews in the Shechem area in central Palestine who had never been to Egypt or taken part in the Exodus. Shechem, the capitol of this region, was situated between Mt. Ebal and Mt. Gerizim. There is nothing in the Bible about Joshua conquering this area. Yet it was the scene for the gathering of the tribes for the covenant ceremonies (Joshua 8:30-35). Joshua built an altar of stones which were unhewn and sacrificed peace offerings. He wrote there upon the stones a copy of the law of Moses in the presence of the children of Israel. On either side of the Ark stood the elders, priests, judges, officers, as well as the stranger and he that was born among them.

He read all the words of Moses to the entire congregation including women, children, and the strangers.

There is archaeological evidence that during the thirteenth century the Israelites conquered cities in Canaan and took possession of the land. Arad is mentioned in the list of cities Joshua conquered (Joshua 12:14).

They occupied the ruined cities like squatters. There is a marked deterioration in pottery; saucer bowls have been found that are very crude. The nomads had settled down but had not yet developed into skillful potters. Village type pottery was found at Hazor about the twelfth century B.C. above the ruins of a Canaanite city. There were small patches of pebble or stone pavements that were not connected with any building remains. Similar paved patches were found on a high terrace of the acropolis of Tel Gat, the same kind of pottery, and no building remains connected with it. Three kilometers north of Tiberius, at Tell Raqqat, similar remains were found. Evidently such squatting of Israelite settlers was common in the late thirteenth century and early twelfth century B.C. Dr. Y. Aharoni found Israelite settlements in the high mountains of central Galilee, one stratum from the thirteenth century, the other the beginning of the twelfth. This was a densely settled Canaanite area, and the new Israelite settlers who wanted to farm had to carve out new agricultural areas in the forests of Central Galilee. On bedrock was the thirteenth-century settlement, whose rough village type pottery dated it. There was a small workshop for smelting and casting metal. The place was deserted until the Middle Israelite period about 970 B.C. and showed remains of a small fortress with casemate walls. By the end of the twelfth century Israel had a foothold in the Promised Land.

CHAPTER XII

THE ISRAELITES SETTLE IN CANAAN

THE ISRAELITES began their occupation of the promised land as squatters in the ruins of their captured cities, or as small farmers and smiths in the mountains. They ate from thick, handmade pottery, drank from wineskins, and dug the soil with stone axes and mattocks. The isolation of the hill country where they first entrenched themselves removed them from the path of the conquerors of the Early Iron Age, the Egyptians and the Hittites.

In the fourteenth century B.C. these two great powers fought each other with mercenary troops from the barbarian hinterlands. They replaced native troops who had either been killed off or debauched by plunder. Who these barbarians were can be learned from carvings on the walls of Karnak and Luxor, where Ramses II celebrated his escape from a Hittite ambush at the battle of Kadesh about 1295 B.C. The Hittites used mercenaries from Cilicia in Asia Minor and Dardanians from the Balkan Peninsula. These people appeared later on in the invasion of the Sea Peoples. The Egyptian mercenaries were Sardinians, Libyans, Nubians, who in later centuries were Pharaohs. The mercenaries were quick to learn the arts of civilization from their masters, especially the secret of working iron for the making of weapons. Eventually these barbarians turned these weapons on the Egyptians and Hittites and caused their downfall.

Now the Egyptians were finding plenty to plunder in Canaan, still rich from the Hyksos boom. When the Egyptian pharaoh began the siege of Megiddo it was during the wheat harvest. He commandeered over 450,000 bushels of wheat, 20,000 sheep and 2,000 goats. Those were the days when the rich Canaanite princes of Megiddo slept in beds inlaid with ivory, traveled in ivory-inlaid sedan chairs, and carried walking sticks. During the excavation of Megiddo by the Oriental Institute of Chicago some of these ivory carvings were found hidden in a room. Megiddo's water tunnel was an engineering masterpiece, and still can be walked through in Israel. The shaft is sunk through solid rock, and steps lead down to a spring which in ancient times supplied the city with water.

One of the most massive Canaanite temples was located at Megiddo in the twelfth century. It was several stories high. Similar temples were built to Baal and Dagon in Ugarit in Syria which was the seat of Canaanite learning. Archaeologists found a huge library of cuneiform clay tablets at Ugarit. Here, learned priests instructed scribes how to write religious texts, as well as business documents and medical lore. These tablets revealed the myths, epics, and legends of the Canaanite religion.

The Canaanite religion was concerned with the fertility of crops, herds and family. The Canaanites practiced sacred prostitution, and this was not only forbidden in Israel but was an abomination (Deuteronomy 23:17-19). "There shall be no cult prostitute of the daughters of Israel, neither shall there be a cult prostitute of the sons of Israel. You shall not bring the hire of a harlot, or the wages of a dog into the house of the Lord your God in payment of any vow; for both these are an abomination to the Lord your God."

The religion of Israel demanded adherence to a stern code of ethics and the belief in a God who stood alone with no other gods on his level.

The Canaanite religion had a whole pantheon of gods and goddesses. The chief god was "El," often represented in art by a bull. He was the father bull, the father of years, the creator of creatures. His wife was called "Lady Asherah of the Sea" and was the mother of the gods. Their son was Baal, the rain and fertility god, "the rider of the clouds," and their daughter was Anath, who was also Baal's wife. The enemy of Baal was Mot, the god of death.

Courtesy Louvre

Baal the Storm God astride a bull with lightning bolts in his hand.

The Ugaritic poems about Baal and Anath symbolize nature. In the dry summer when there is no rain, Baal dies. The poem reads:

> "The Puissant Baal has died,
> That the Prince, Lord of Earth, had perished."

The poem continues:

> "Then Anath the Lass draws nigh him.
> Like the heart of a cow for her calf,
> Like the heart of a ewe for her lamb,
> So's the heart of Anath for Baal.
> She seizes the Godly Mot—
> With sword she doth cleave him—
> With fan she doth winnow him—
> With fire she doth burn him.
> With hand-mill she grinds him—
> In the fields she doth sow him."

This is symbolic of the fall planting. Then the winter rains soak the earth and in the spring the earth is green, the cows drop their young, and Baal comes to life, is resurrected and marries again the fertility goddess Anath. This myth of the dying-reborn god was familiar in the Near East. In Babylonia Tammuz died and was resurrected to marry the fertility goddess, Ishtar. In Egypt, Osiris, the sun, died and was reborn to marry Isis. In Greece the myth applies to Adonis and Aphrodite.

H. L. Ginsberg discovered a number of archaic Hebrew words in Ugaritic which clarified the meaning of many Biblical passages when translated from Hebrew. Psalms 68.4 was written: "Extol him that rideth upon the skies, whose name is the Lord . . ." In the translation from Ugaritic it reads: "Extol him the rider of the clouds. . . ." Baal is called Zabul, the exalted, Lord of Earth, Lord of Heaven and the Rider of the Clouds. Baal as a god of the storm had a loud voice, thunder. In Exodus 19:16 we read, "And it came to pass on the third day when it was morning, that there were thunders and lightnings, and a thick cloud upon the mount, and the voice of a horn exceedingly loud; and all the people that were in the camp trembled. And Moses brought forth the people out of the camp to meet God." Yahweh as a God of Thunder and Lightning is described in Psalms 18:8

"Then the earth did shake and quake,
The foundations also of the mountains did tremble;
They were shaken because He was wroth."

Baal in the Canaanite religion was also the creator, the preserver, the protector of the world and Psalms 29:7-9 ascribes to the Lord glory and strength.

The poetic form of these stories is similar to the poetry of the Hebrew Psalms. Psalms 92:9 reads:

"For lo, Thine enemies, O Lord,
For, lo, Thine enemies shall perish;

All the workers of iniquity shall be scattered."

Psalms 145:13 reads:

"Thy Kingdom is a kingdom for all ages,
And thy dominion endureth throughout all generations."

The Baal myth reads:

"Now thine enemy O Baal
Now thine enemy wilt thou smite,
Now wilt thou cut off thine adversary,
Thou'lt take thine eternal kingdom,
Thine everlasting dominion."

Canaanite temples excavated at Ugarit and at Bethshan in Palestine, which date from the fourteenth to the tenth century, are similar in plan to Solomon's Temple. The main room was entered through an indirect entrance for it was not considered proper for the curious to look directly into the temple. The ceiling was held up by two columns. Around the room was a low bench where offerings were placed. A series of steps led up to an inner room, "Holy of Holies," where in Canaanite temples the god's statue was kept on a raised platform. Before the steps was an altar for incense and offerings.

Usually sacrifices were fired on an altar outside the building. In the debris around an altar in front of a temple excavated at Lachish were found bones of goats, sheep, and oxen. All the

Courtesy Israel Department of Antiquities

Modern cast made from clay mold of a Canaanite Goddess.

animals were young, and the bones were from the upper part of the foreleg. H. Ernest Wright uses these archaeological remains to show the similarity between Hebrew and Canaanite ritual. Leviticus 7:32 reads: "And the right thigh shall ye give unto the priest for a heave offering out of your sacrifices of peace offerings." Only boneless fat was to be burned on the altar. Only the priest's portion was found inside the temple. Few of the bones showed evidence of burning, so the meat may have been boiled or cooked outside the temple. The worshippers ate the sacrifice outside the temple, as a rule.

In 1947 a Canaanite temple of the sixteenth century was discovered by Dr. I. Ben-Dor on the seashore at Nehariyya in Galilee. This was originally a high place. Later on a large rectangular temple was erected. In the courtyard were the remains of a stone altar. Later on rooms were added to the structure. The goddess worshipped at this shrine has been reproduced from half of a mold, found on the site. Votive offerings consisted of bronze, silver and gold jewelry, semi-precious stone beads, silver strips with lightly chased images of the goddess, pottery figurines of

Courtesy Israel Department of Antiquities

Three-legged bird figurine Myceneaen importation found in late Canaanite tomb.

animals and birds, small pots, and tumblers used for libation vessels.

This sacred area was apparently connected with a sweet water spring. The whole site had sunk below the water level, and the discovery was accidental.

The dead were buried in family graves, as we have seen from the tombs of Jericho during Hyksos times, and provided with all necessities for the next world. The Angel of Death was Sheol in the Netherworld, Isaiah 5:14: "Therefore the netherworld hath enlarged her desire, and opened her mouth without measure."

Influence of Canaanite Religion on the Israelites

By the end of the thirteenth century the Israelites had settled in the hill country on both sides of the Jordan. The invention of lime-plastered cisterns greatly aided the settlement. These waterproof cisterns caught and stored rain water, so that the Israelites were not wholly dependent on perennial streams or springs. As the population increased rapidly, these semi-nomads quickly settled in farming villages. At Bethel and Tell Beit Mirsim, Israelites, who were free men, occupied the ground floors of mansions of Canaanite patricians. Gone were the feudal days when farmers worked for the lord without pay. In the rain-hungry country they worshipped Baal and Ashtoreth. Some clay plaques have been found made in molds of a nude woman with a distended abdomen, to which both hands are convulsively pressed as if she is about to give birth. She wears none of the decorations of Canaanite goddesses. There has never been found a statue of Yahweh. Ashtoreth figurines were found at Arad at a tenth century B.C. level along with a Hebrew seal.

From Judges 2:11 and onward, this sentence appears continually, "And the children of Israel did that which was evil in the sight of the Lord and served the Baalim."

It is evident the mass of people gave Yahweh the attributes of Baal. He was a rain god, an agricultural god, a fertility god. He was worshipped at Canaanite high places, and as we saw at Lachish, the sacrificial ritual of Canaan was borrowed. Even

Courtesy Israel Department of Antiquities

Israelite figurine of Ashtoreth.

leaders like King David and King Solomon were tolerant of figurines and Baal worshippers.

The first Israelite literary composition, the Song of Deborah, may have been influenced by the victory hymns so popular at that time. On the walls of the Temple of Karnak are the annals of Thutmose III's military campaigns in Palestine:

"Now two roads are here.
One of the roads is to the east of us,
So that it comes out at Ta'anach.
Behold the other, is to the north of Djefti,
And we will come out to the north of Megiddo."

The Biblical poem, Song of Deborah, reads:

"The kings came, they fought;
Then fought the kings of Canaan,
In Taanach by the waters of Megiddo . . ."

The poet tells of the place where the battle took place but gives credit to Yahweh for victory in contrast to the Egyptian kings who bragged of their victories and conceived of no greater power than they.

The tribes of Is'sachar, Zebulun, Naphtali, Ephraim, Benjamin and Machir were rallied to the standard of Yahweh to fight the enemy under the command of Barak of Issachar. The other tribes did not fight, which shows there was not yet a feeling of nationalism among the tribes. The poet asks of Reuben,

"Why did you tarry among the sheepfolds
To hear the pipings of the flocks?
Among the clans of Reuben
There were great searchings of the heart?

The battle is vividly described:

"Then did the horsehoofs stamp
By reason of the prancings, the prancings
Of the mighty ones."

A woman named Jael saved Israel. When the general Sisera came to her tent asking for water,

"Milk she gave him. In a lordly bowl she brought him curd.
Her hand she put to the tent pin,
And her right hand to the workman's hammer.
She struck Sisera a blow
She crushed his head
She shattered and pierced his temple
He sank, he fell,
He lay still at her feet."

The poem ends ironically, pointing out the immorality of the Canaanites debauched with booty. Sisera's mother peered through the lattice of her window and asked,

"Why is his chariot so long in coming?
Are they not finding, are they not dividing the spoil?
A damsel, two damsels to every man;
To Sisera a spoil of dyed garments,
A spoil of dyed garments of embroidery,
Two dyed garments of 'broidery
For the neck of every spoiler!"

The last line of the poem reads:

"So perish all Thine enemies O Lord;
But they that love Him be as the sun
When he goeth forth in his might."

This was the difference between Canaan and Israel as seen through the eyes of the poet.

After this victory the land was peaceful for forty years. Then, Judges, Chapter 6, begins, "And the Children of Israel did that which was evil in the sight of the Lord, and the Lord delivered them into the hand of the Midian for seven years." Another hero, Gideon, rescued them. After Gideon died, they went astray and made Baal-berith their god.

The Book of Judges is full of barbaric incidents, like Jephthah, the Gileadite, who was a mighty man but the son of a harlot. Jephthah asked God to give him victory and promised to sacrifice the first thing he met after his victory. He met his daughter and sacrificed her according to his vow. After that it was the custom for the women of Israel to mourn Jephthah's daughter four days in a year. The Book of Judges ends, "In those days there was no king in Israel, and every man did that which was right in his own eyes." Every man had to learn for himself the righteousness and power of God.

The Coming of the Philistines

The year 1200 B.C. was a dark age for the great civilizations of Asia and Egypt. An invasion of the Sea Peoples from the north Mediterranean coasts and islands, destroyed the Hittite empire in Asia Minor and drove the Canaanites out of the coastal plains of Palestine. They came in boats with one end abruptly turned up and the other a ramming point. On land they travelled with heavy, two-wheeled, ox-drawn carts containing their possessions, their women, and their children. Whole populations were looking for new homes in Asia. Ramses III turned them back at Djahi, which he celebrated in a victory poem. This victory lasted only during his lifetime, for these invaders ended the Egyptian empire in Asia. The decline of Egypt began from this period. This was a dark age for a large part of the civilized world. The Mycenean civilization in Greece was wiped out. The Kassite Empire in Babylonia tottered and became subject to Assyrian overlords.

Some of these Palestine invaders were refugees from the Dorian invasion of Greece, the siege of Troy, and the reshuffling of power in the Mycenean and Aegean islands. They settled along the coastal plain of Palestine and are known in the Bible as the Philistines. They were ruled by the five city states of Gaza, Ashkelon, Ashdod, Ekron, and Gath. The rulers had the Mycenean name of "sarens" or "tyrant." The Philistines had theaters and a building like a Greek "Megaron," which is a large rectangular hall with a circular hearth in the center, which was sacred to Demeter. The Philistines adopted the Canaanite god Dagon. During the invasion the Israelites were ignored and given a chance to consolidate themselves in the hills.

Once the Philistines were entrenched, they began to harass the Israelites with their superior weapons: chariots and iron. The Israelites had iron but did not know how to work it. A. L. Kroeber has described iron as the great "democratizing agent." Bronze was expensive, and the metal of kings, but iron, which was cheap and abundant, was the metal of the common man. The invention of the bellows around 1500 B.C. hastened the production of iron in quantities. Iron could be used by everybody for plowshares, farm tools, and kettles. Steelmaking gave the Philistines superior swords.

The Bible gives us a picture of this superiority in the stories of Samson. Tortured and blinded by the Philistines, with a last burst of strength he pulled down the pillars of their temple of Dagon.

About 1080 B.C. the Philistines extended their rule to the hill country. Excavation at Ashdod revealed it to be the center of pottery manufacture and the site of the temple of Dagon. Their pottery was painted light red to buff in color. The designs are reminiscent of Aegean pottery, stylized birds, spirals, interlocking semicircles; the shapes are pitchers with short necks and painted bottoms, long necked jars with globular bottoms.

The fall of Shiloh and the capture of the Ark of the Covenant by the Philistines about 1050 B.C. was the lowest ebb in the history of the loosely confederated Israelite tribes. They needed a leader to unite them so they could recapture the sacred Ark. The Bible tells us, the Philistines brought the Ark to the house of Dagon at Ashdod (I Samuel 5:3). "When they of Ashdod arose early on the morrow, behold, Dagon was fallen upon his face to the ground before the Ark of the Lord." The Philistines had so much trouble with the Ark in their land that they returned it to Israel. It remained in Kiriath-jearim until the times of King David.

In the meantime Saul became the first king of Israel. He led a revolt against the Philistines and was defeated on Mount Gilboa. He had welded the tribes and their chieftains into a nation and had thrust the Philistines out of the hills.

W. F. Albright excavated the citadel of Saul at Gibeah on the summit of Tell el-Ful in 1922-33. All that survived was a corner tower and a casemate wall. This type of wall was originated in the Late Bronze Age in Asia Minor by the Hittites, who spread it to Syria; from Syria it was brought to Palestine. For example, two walls were constructed running parallel to each other, with the distance between of 6 feet. The space between the walls was divided into long narrow rooms. In fortresses these rooms were filled with stones and earth, plastered over, and made into one thick strong wall. Some of these rooms were left empty, used as storerooms, and connected by doors with the interior of the fortress. Casemate walls were found in the excavations of Tell Beit Mirsim and Beth-shemesh, which date to the early part of David's reign about the beginning of the tenth century.

David defeated the Philistines, and so reduced their power and territory that they were never a threat to Israel again. Before we consider the glorious reign of King David, let us look to the north at the new kingdom of Phoenicia.

The Phoenicians

The rise of Phoenicia and the eclipse of Egypt is told in a story written about 1100 B.C. The Egyptian priests who were now in power sent the writer of the story, Wen-Amon, to Byblos in Syria for cedar wood. On the way Wen-Amon was robbed of his credentials and gold and silver. Zakar-Baal, the Prince of Byblos, not only refused to receive the Egyptian but sent his harbor master with the command, "Get out of my harbor!"

Wen-Amon tried to impress the Prince with the power and majesty of Egypt, who had controlled the trade of Byblos since the days of the Old Kingdom, by telling the Phoenician that Amon-Re, king of gods, needed the timber.

Prince Zakar-Baal answered he was not subject to Egypt, and unless he was paid in gold he would not sell Egypt any cedar wood. He agreed, "Now Amon has founded all lands. He founded them, but first he founded the land of Egypt from which you come; for skill came out of it, to reach the place where I am. What then are these silly trips which they have had you make?"

The Egyptian finally convinced Zakar-Baal to send cedar timbers in advance of payment. Egypt sent in exchange jars of gold and silver, fine linen, 500 rolls of commercial papyrus, ox-hides, ropes, sacks of lentils, and baskets of fish. The prestige of Egypt was a thing of the past. Phoenicia ruled the commerce of the Mediterranean. The Nora Stone from Sardinia has inscriptions in Phoenician script showing that Sardinia was a Phoenician colony by the ninth century B.C. The Phoenicians founded Carthage in North Africa. Pottery found in tombs is related to Megiddo pottery of the tenth century. Phoenician ivories found at Carmona in southwestern Spain resemble the twelfth-century Megiddo ivories and those found at Samaria in the ninth century.

We shall see how Phoenician art and civilization influenced the monarchy of Israel. Their greatest invention was the alphabet.

The Phoenicians are given credit for inventing purely phonetic writing which expresses only sounds, and does not contain pictures and symbols. The alphabet was adopted by the Israelites.

This alphabet was taken over by the Greeks, who added vowels, and later by the Latins, whose alphabet we use. The alphabet put reading and writing within the grasp of the common man. It could be learned in hours, and a man could learn to write in weeks compared to the months and years required to learn to write cuneiform or Egyptian hieroglyphics. Small traders could keep accounts they could read, and the average citizen could afford a tomb inscription. By the eighth century a prophet like Amos, who was a shepherd, became the first prophetic writer.

Another commercial people who influenced Israel were the Aramaeans, Semites of the same group as the Hebrews. They established themselves inland at Damascus. They had their own versions of weights and measures, writing and language. Assyria was half Aramaic-speaking at the time of its fall. Aramaic was used in Persia, and became the everyday language of Palestine in the days of Jesus. The Aramaean alphabet influenced those of Persia, India, the Jews, Arabs, the Nestorian Christians, the ancient Turks, the Mongols, and the Manchus.

CHAPTER XIII

THE UNITED MONARCHY OF DAVID AND SOLOMON

FOUR HUNDRED YEARS from the time Moses united some loosely related tribes into a people with a covenant with God, King David united these people into a monarchy that extended from the borders of Egypt to the Euphrates. He subdued the Philistines, conquered Moab, Ammon, Edom, and Damascus, making Israel the most powerful smaller state between the great powers in Mesopotamia and Egypt.

It was an auspicious time for the farmers and herdsmen of the hill country to rule Palestine. The Kassite kingdom of Babylonia had fallen before a rising new power, Assyria, under Tiglath-pileser I (1115-1100 B.C.). The Assyrians were busy subduing their immediate neighbors and extending their boundaries to the Black Sea. They would not become a threat to Israel until the ninth century B.C. Egypt was going into eclipse. It began after the heretic king Ikhnaton had tried to change the religion to "One Sun God," and neglected the empire in Palestine and Syria. Then followed the scandal of tomb robberies, engineered by high officials. Mummies of ancient pharaohs were found strewn in the desert, and all the gold, silver, and precious furniture was stolen from their tombs. Eventually these royal gods were gathered up and stacked like cordwood in a secret tomb. After the peoples of the sea had been checked, a Libyan became Pharaoh. He was followed by a Nubian ruler. The sudden collapse of the Hittite empire in 1150 B.C. cut off Egypt's supply of iron, which had replaced copper as the new basic metal of the world economy. It is significant that Egypt no longer exploited the Sinai copper mines so that later on in Solomon's reign (ca. 970-940 B.C.) the Israel mines in the Wadi Arabah supplied the world with copper. The new commercial power to the north, Phoenicia, was friendly to Israel.

David's strategy to capture Jerusalem united the ten tribes to the north with the two tribes he ruled from Hebron. The murder of Saul's son Ishbaal, who had ruled the north, brought notables from the north who formally and publicly proclaimed David king over the entire nation.

Jerusalem was considered impregnable. Subsequent history will show the difficulties of the Assyrians, the Babylonians, and even the Romans in conquering it. This city not only lay on the central ridge, the most convenient route north and south through the hill country, but the great highways connecting the Mediterranean with Mesopotamia and Egypt were not too far away.

David's general Joab entered Jerusalem through an underground tunnel. A vertical shaft inside the city gave access to the water through this tunnel in time of siege. Joab crawled up the shaft into the Jebusite city, where he created so much pandemonium among the Jebusites that David was able to break into the city and capture it.

David gave to Jerusalem the sacred name of "The City of God." David returned the "Ark" to Jerusalem from where it had been kept in the house of Obed-edom, a Philistine in David's service. The superstitious Philistines allowed him to move the Ark to Jerusalem because they hoped to share in the divine blessings. David, robed in the linen vestments worn by the priests, danced with the marchers as they followed the sacred chest to the palace. David selected a site for a temple to house the Ark. Thus Jerusalem become the religious center.

David modelled his administration on that of Egypt. Besides lists of officials, the Bible describes two other officers, Jehoshaphat the recorder, who was in charge of archives; and a Royal Herald, who regulated ceremonies in the palace and was the intermediary between the king and the people. David also had a scribe with an Egyptian name. It is possible he did not come from Egypt but from Phoenicia, where the alphabet was the same as that used in Israel.

With the aid of Phoenician workmen David strengthened the fortifications of Jerusalem, built himself a palace, repaired the Tabernacle, and placed within it the Ark of the Covenant. From David's reign Jerusalem was the religious center of Israel.

There is practically no archaeological evidence of David's reign. Much of Israelite Jerusalem lies under the modern Jerusalem. The contours of the ground have been changed by continuous building operations, the tearing up of walls of earlier buildings, as well as vast piles of rubbish deposits.

For Solomon's reign there is no evidence in Jerusalem but there is a great deal of archaeological evidence in Megiddo, Hazor, Gezer, and Arad. In modern Jerusalem on the Jordan side, the Moslem sanctuary, the Haram esh-Sherif, called The Dome of the Rock, covers the site of Solomon's Temple. The Temple lay west of the sacred rock covered by the Dome. This rock may have been the altar of sacrifices. The construction of the Temple must have required terracing and massive retaining walls for the great courtyard. Solomon's palace was a succession of courts, like buildings found in Mesopotamia, and was located south of the Temple.

The dimensions of the Temple are described in the Bible, and we know it to be a triple building with a holy of holies, a hall, a porch in front, and also side chambers in three stories. There has been some question whether the bronze pillars in front were free standing, or formed part of the architectural facade.

There is no doubt that Solomon's temple was a typical Phoenician temple. A ninth-century temple has been excavated at Tell Tainat in Syria and has the same main structure but no side chambers. In the Hazor excavations there is the same triple form with a porch, but somewhat narrower. In Ras Shamra a courtyard wall was found using brick or stone with wood, like the description in I Kings 6:36 that the Temple courtyard was built "with three courses of hewn stone and a course of ceder beams."

The Phoenician architects copied the clerestory windows from the Egyptians who lighted a room from windows under the ceiling, above the side rooms and around the main room. This clerestory type of lighting of the Egyptians was used by the Greeks and Romans and came down to our modern cathedrals.

The decorations of carved palm trees, flowers and gold leaf

have parallels in fragments of ivory carvings found at Megiddo and Samaria. The cherubim looked like winged Sphinxes.

Gateways at Megiddo, Gezer, and Hazor date to Solomon's period. They are all imposing with an internal entrance passage flanked by four guardrooms in a row. The casemate walls are similar. A casemate wall is widened by a succession of rooms inside the wall which strengthen it and are used for storage.

Megiddo was one of the most elaborate of Solomon's fortresses, surrounded by a wall eleven feet thick. This was where he supposedly kept his horses. The horses were tied to hitching posts, which also held up the ceiling of the building.

At Tell Arad, a tenth-century fortress dates to the days of Solomon and has the casemate walls like those mentioned above. Arad dominated the road to the Arabah, Edom, and Elath where Solomon had his copper working industry. In the 1930's Nelson Glueck and the American School of Oriental Research in Jerusalem carried out a systematic survey of the Negev. This revealed a wealth of sites where mining and smelting of copper were done. Along the eastern bank of the Arabah was found rock containing veins of copper and iron ore. This was mined by Solomon. The ore was given a preliminary smelting in small furnaces near the mines. There were walled enclosures near the slag heaps that contained ruins of miners' huts and smelting furnaces. It is probable these were prison camps, the mines worked by slave labor, both in Solomon's time and later by the Edomites. This is in the midst of the desert where the heat is extreme in the summer, and water has to be brought in from miles away. No freeborn Israelite would work there, unless he were forced to. Nelson Glueck also found a large tenth-century B.C. smelting refinery at Ezion-geber. This was a large building whose rooms had walls with specially prepared holes in them. The upper row of holes opened into a system of air channels which ran through the main walls. The building was obviously a smelter because these were flues. The ore which had been smelted at the mines was brought here in crucibles and put inside the smelter. The room was filled with wood and brush and fired. The draft from the flues made the fire hot enough to refine the metal to the point where it could be worked into ingots for shipment. Furnaces in Palestine remelted the metal, and it was cast or beaten into implements. The walls of the refinery were stained green from the copper. The refinery was placed in the path of the winds that blow with fury down the Arabah from the north. The flues of the smelter were turned toward the north, so there was no need of bellows or forced draft. Here also, at Ezion-geber, Glueck discovered Solomon's seaport, where Hiram of Tyre built for him the fleet that traded as far as Ethiopia.

Whether under the Israelites or the Edomites, Ezion-geber remained an important harbor for five centuries. The settlement was rebuilt three times. This port gives us a glimpse at another source of Solomon's great wealth that was expended in making Jerusalem so magnificent.

Archaeology does reveal the comparative poverty of the small towns of Israel in contrast to the splendor of Jerusalem. Solomon lost his copper mines to Edom before he died, which was one cause of the disintegration of his kingdom. The other causes were his tolerance of foreign gods and the fierce opposition of those faithful to Yahweh, his enslavement of the working classes, and heavy taxation. He died in 935 B.C. By 930 B.C. the northern tribes under the leadership of Jeroboam had revolted against Solomon's successor Rehoboam.

The United Monarchy had its faults, but it also had its glory and brought the civilized world to Israel. From this period begin the literary works that ultimately became the Holy Bible.

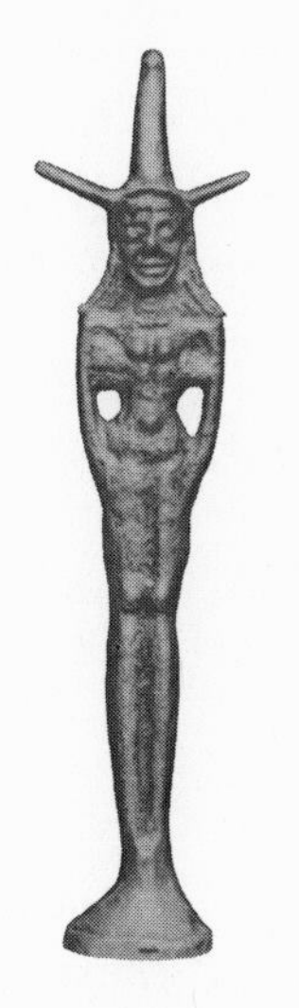

CHAPTER XIV

LIFE OF THE PEOPLE DURING THE MONARCHY

THE BIBLE TELLS US of the splendor of Solomon's palaces and the magnificence in which he lived I Kings 10:4-7. "And when the queen of Sheba had seen all the wisdom of Solomon, and the house he had built, and the food of his table, and the sitting of his servants, and the attendance of his ministers and their apparel, and his cup-bearers, and his burnt-offering which he offered in the name of the Lord, there was no spirit in her. And she said to the King, 'It was a true report that I heard in mine own land of thine acts, and of thy wisdom.' "

Archaeology has unearthed the life of the people. At the beginning of the twentieth century Macalister found the famous Gezer Calendar while excavating Gezer. This is the oldest Israelite inscription yet found from the late tenth century. It is a schoolboy's exercise tablet made of soft limestone, 4 inches long and 2 inches wide. On this soft stone was the order of the agricultural seasons.

Let us imagine the boy was called Ahijah, the name scratched on the calendar, and was about fourteen years old. His chest was bare and he wore a knee-length, linen, wraparound skirt or waistcloth which he held in place with a leather belt. In cold weather he covered his chest with a shirt. If it was very cold he put on a sheepskin. His hair was short, and he went barefoot. The bottoms of his feet were as tough as leather from walking in the fields helping his father plow for the planting of grain. The plow, pulled by a bullock, was a piece of wood with an iron tip. It just cut furrows in the soil three or four inches deep and is still used in the Near East by backward peoples today. As he plowed he sang,

"His two months are olive harvest;
His two months are planting grain;
His two months are late planting;
His month is hoeing up the flax;
His month is harvest of the barley;
His month is harvest and festivity;
His two months are vine-tending;
His month is summer fruit."

"You can sing the calendar, can you write it?" challenged his younger sister Rachel, who was driving their small herd of milk goats to pasture in the olive orchard. She wore a long linen blue tunic, and her thick brown hair hung in two braids with bangs over her forehead. She, too, was barefooted.

"Sure, I can write it," answered Ahijah, as he stopped the

Courtesy Israel Department of Antiquities

Modern Bedouin plow not very different from plow used in Israelite times.

bullock to remove a large stone, one of the many stones glaciers had strewn over the Judean hills in the dim past. "When we go home at sundown I'll show you."

"Will you teach me to write, Ahijah?" asked Rachel wistfully.

"Your mother will teach you all your duties as a wife and housekeeper," said their father, who took the plow away from Ahijah and told him to scratch into the ground with a hoe the seeds which had just been scattered in the furrows.

Their father shook his head as he watched Rachel running after the goats. Wasn't it enough of a chore for a father to teach his sons reading and writing without bothering with daughters? Ahijah was the youngest of four sons, to whom he had taught the history of their forefathers and the divine commands of God to obey the law. He patiently told them the stories of their forefathers, gave explanations, and asked questions. Ahijah repeated the stories very well, answered most of the questions, and asked some questions like, "Why must I know the farmer's calendar?"

"You must learn to be a farmer if you want to follow in my footsteps," his father had answered. It was the duty of every Israelite father to teach his son a trade or profession unless he wanted him to grow up to be a thief. Trades were hereditary, boys followed their father's trade. If Ahijah had a talent for writing, he might learn to be a scribe and even go to the court of the king as a secretary. If he was really hungry for knowledge he could join a group which gathered around a prophet or teacher of wisdom and be trained in the law.

When the day's work was done Ahijah and his father climbed the hill to their home behind the walls of Gezer. Some of the farmers lived in a village just outside the walls of the city. There was now peace in the land with Solomon as king; farmers were no longer fearful that an enemy would attack and burn the city.

Ahijah's father explained to him that Gezer was one of the finest cities in Israel. The Pharaoh of Egypt had made a present of the city of Gezer to King Solomon when he married the Pharaoh's daughter. True, the city had been destroyed when Solomon received it. He had rebuilt the walls with carefully hewn and fitted stones. "Look," Ahijah's father tried to insert between the stones the blade of his iron knife he carried in his leather belt. "These walls are strong. My knife finds no opening!"

To enter the city, they went into a long passageway with four guardrooms where soldiers with chariots stood guard. As the soldiers nodded for them to pass, Ahijah wished he could be a charioteer and drive the beautiful horses. Gezer was one of King Solomon's fortified cities where he kept chariots. The others were Megiddo, Lower Beth-horon, Baalath, Tamar.

"I wish I could be a soldier, wear a beautiful bronze helmet, and carry a shining bronze shield," said Ahijah.

"In battle you'd carry a thick, leather shield covered with fat, and a leather helmet," said his father. "These charioteers are not freemen; they serve directly under the king and are Solomon's men."

"Some of them were given land by the king," said Ahijah. "One soldier told me he did not have to pay taxes and would never be forced to work for the king."

"When the king dies all these men will belong to Solomon's son who becomes king," said his father. "King David's professional soldiers, the 'runners,' now belong to Solomon. As a farmer you are a free man."

They made a right turn into the city. There in front of the gate was the marketplace, where potters, jewelers, cabinet makers, weavers, sandal makers were selling their wares. Ahijah went to the produce section where his mother and two older sisters were selling fresh vegetables from their garden. His father stopped to look at some fat-tailed sheep another farmer had for sale. Fat-tails of sheep were considered a great delicacy in those days.

Then everybody was attracted to an argument right in front of the city gates, where lawsuits were held and commercial transactions arranged. Ahijah dived through the crowd to the first row where he would not miss anything. A farmer was shouting at a judge who had ordered him to deliver as part of his taxes some of his stored grain to feed the king's horses.

"Those horses live better than we do," the man was shouting. "Each one has a roof over his head and his own stall, with every stone laid perfectly; and each horse tied to a stone hitching post with a perfectly cut hole. I know because my son is a stone cutter and was forced to work on that stable!"

"Calm down, Ephraim," Ahijah's father had put his hand on

the farmer's shoulder. "Give them the grain or you may be forced to quarry stone for the king."

The farmer's shoulders slumped as he agreed to deliver some of his grain to the stables for the horses. Ahijah listened to him complain as he walked home with his father. "The king is in the business of buying and selling horses. These horses the Hurrians breed on the steppes of Cilicia bring high prices, and the king becomes rich, not the nation."

Ahijah's father did not reply, because he was a man who was loyal to the king. He was satisfied with his comfortable house near the old casemate wall of the city.

Ahijah ran into the kitchen on the ground floor of the house where he smelled freshly baked unleavened round cakes which his grandmother had just baked. She had just set a pot of chick peas in the fire of a small round oven on the floor. The oven was made of four wide overlapping strips of clay and broken pieces of pottery. She was annoyed at Ahijah, who snatched a cake off one of the curved trays she had just removed from the hot coals in the oven. "Look out, you'll burn yourself, Ahijah!" He stumbled against some huge storage jars and bins against the walls where grain was stored and rattled the pottery dishes and jugs on a shelf. Ahijah did knock over a jar of water which broke; and the water drained into a cistern underneath the floor. Every drop of water was saved and used for the goats who were housed in the courtyard in front of the house, and for the small vegetable garden whose produce his mother sometimes sold to the wealthy wives of officials who lived in the large houses in the new section of town.

"Run to the spring and bring more water, Ahijah," his grandmother commanded. "Hurry before it gets dark." She sat down on a straw mat and began to pound some grain for more cakes in a stone bowl with a stone pestle and grumbled, "I hope the rainy season comes soon and fills those cisterns on the roof. Then we won't be so dependent on the spring for water."

Ahijah did hurry because it was almost sundown and the water tunnel was dark, even if there were pinch-lipped oil lamps burning in niches. The spring was 130 feet down from the street and he had to walk down steps at an angle of about 39 degrees, almost straight up and down. It was fun following some pretty girls down the steps to the spring. At the bottom he drank deeply of the pure

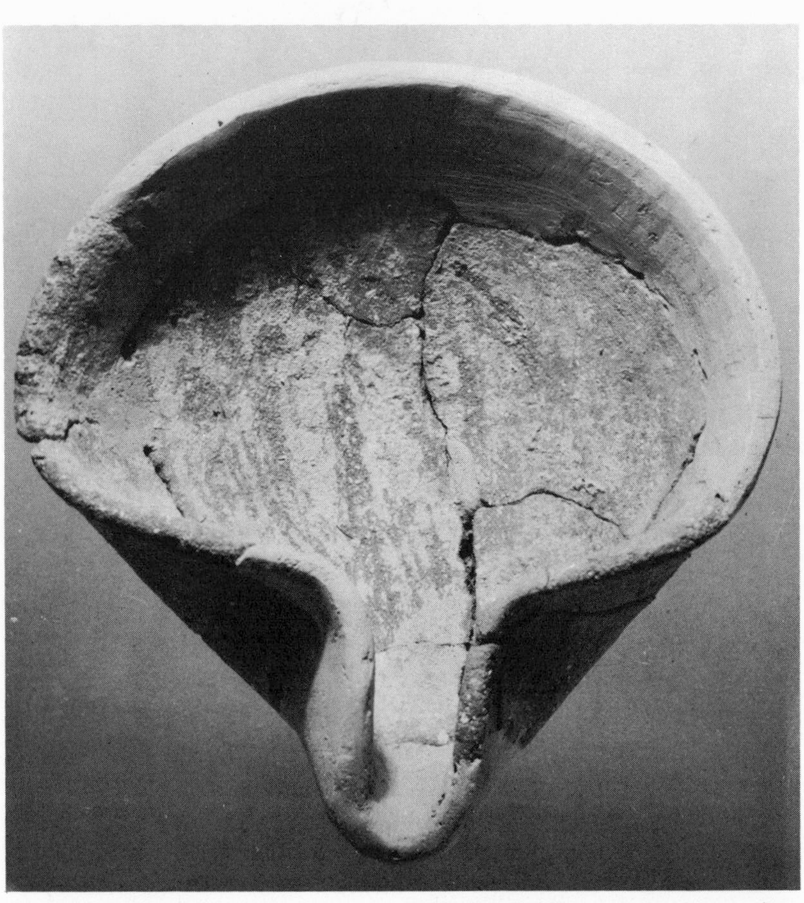

Courtesy Israel Department of Antiquities

Pinch-lipped oil lamp used for illumination in Israelite times.

artesian water. Then he raised the jug full of water on his shoulder and climbed to the street. He had to walk slowly so as not to spill the water, and this gave him a chance to peek into the courtyards of the rich elders and chiefs. Through open doors he could see the tables and chairs inside. The houses were all two-storied, and he glanced up to see a beautiful woman resting on a wooden couch by the window of an upstairs room. She wore a lovely long, blue linen tunic, and over it was draped a white robe. A narrow scarf was tied around her head. An older woman in the courtyard told him to stop staring and move on. She was also dressed in an expensive linen dress, made of different colored threads which reminded him of the story he had learned about Joseph and his coat of many colors. In the setting sun it shone blue, red, and gold. He stared at her dress because he had heard his father tell of the city of Debir, in the south on the edge of the desert in the Negev. Here great flocks of sheep were raised. Everybody in that town had a loom and wove woolen cloth. There they knew the secret for the purple dye, from the murex shellfish in the Mediterranean. The Israelites had learned the art of making this cloth from the Canaanites. Now many of the Canaanites were part of Israel and worshipped both Baal and Yahweh. His father had described the dye plants in Debir, of which there were at least twenty. The cloth was put into small stone basins about one and a half feet across with a six-inch opening at the top. These stood in a larger basin about three feet high which caught any of the precious dye which spilled out of the smaller basin. Large pierced stones were used to press the dye out of the material. Potash and lime were used to fix the dye. In Debir they mostly dyed thread, so that was why they used small dye vats. This cloth was so expensive that King Solomon had requested Hiram, King of Tyre, to send an artisan who knew how to make purple, crimson, and blue fabrics for the veil or curtain of the temple. This expert trained Israelite workmen.

The woman had told him to "Be off!" But Ahijah had really seen the elegant cloth and could now tell his sisters that he even smelled the strongly perfumed oil the woman had on, and that her face was powdered white, her lips painted red, and her lower eyelids colored green. Her hair was parted in the middle and puffed out to frame her face, and hung down on her breast in two thick curls. She wore golden colored sandals, jeweled anklets, bracelets, and rings.

It was dark when Ahijah arrived home with the jar of water. A pottery lamp lighted the room. This was a saucer six inches wide, pinched at one end and filled with olive oil. A flax wick provided enough light to eat supper. The lamps were kept in niches. When his father travelled at night, he carried a torch made of wool. They ate grapes and olives with their meals when they were in season. Barley was their main cereal; they ate meat on special occasions.

Ahijah had to wait until they lay down on straw mats on the

roof before falling asleep to describe the elegant lady. It was pleasant to sleep on the roof under the stars before the weather turned rainy. The roof was protected by a small wall or parapet which was required by law on the roofs of all houses in Israel. Ahijah's father reminded him they had better coat the roof with mud, straw, and lime plaster or rain might leak through the log beams which roofed the house, the way it did last winter. It was a messy job fixing the roof. They rolled the new roof on with round oblong stones.

The craftsmen of Gezer lived on certain streets according to their trade. The potters had their own street, as did the bakers who made the leavened bread for the town, as well as barbers, locksmiths, jewelers and others. The pottery was made on a wheel and was very practical. Certain basic shapes and techniques were used for over 300 years. When fired, the clay was red or a reddish brown color. They painted a line of red or black around the shoulder of a small jar or around the middle of a large one and burnished the pottery so that it came out of the fire with a shining surface. There were royal potteries in the towns of Hebron, Ziph, Socoh, and Memshath, where huge ten-gallon jars were made, with the King's royal stamp to standardize the amount of oil and wine shipped in the jars.

The technology for working gold, copper, iron, lead, and silver was well advanced in Israel. The Israelites were excellent metal workers and jewelers. Some of the ivories found at Samaria and Megiddo were real works of art. But Israel did not produce much art because the country was predominantly agricultural—democratic and not wealthy. Israel produced no great plastic art. Her contribution was religion.

But to return to Ahijah and his family, who were typical Israelites of the monarchy. Their life was regulated by the agricultural calendar because the natural source of income for Israel was grain, wine, and olive oil.

The Passover began the barley harvest, and fifty days later was the Feast of Weeks, which was the "festivity" on the Gezer Calendar. With the grain harvest over, Ahijah and his family made a pilgrimage to the central sanctuary with an offering of the first fruits. This was now in Jerusalem; the city swarmed with pilgrims, and there was great joy and feasting.

Ahijah took care of the lambs and kids his father brought to the great altar for burnt offerings in the courtyard of the temple. The altar was built like a staged Babylonian tower, or ziggurat—three stages, fifteen feet high and thirty feet square. It was called "Harel," meaning mountain of God. Each stage was a ledge. A flight of steps led up to the altar or hearth, which was eighteen feet square with horns projecting from each corner.

A huge bronze bowl, fifteen feet in diameter and seven and one-half feet high, was cast of bronze about three inches thick. This, in II Chronicles 4:4, was called the "Molten Sea" and "stood upon twelve oxen, three looking toward the north, and three looking toward the west, and three looking toward the south, and three looking toward the east."

Ordinarily people like Ahijah's family did not enter the temple. They knew however, that inside there were two winged cherubim, fifteen feet high, overlaid with gold leaf, their wings seven and one-half feet long, their faces inward, guarding the Holy of Holies. They believed that the spirit of God stood on the cherubim, but there was no statue like that of Baal which stood on a bull in the heathen temples Solomon had built for his foreign wives inside the palace grounds.

There was murmuring among the prophets who were allowed to preach in the courtyard. The Lord was punishing Solomon for allowing his wives to worship Baal. Damascus and Amman had revolted and were now independent. The northern tribes were tired of paying heavy taxes in produce or forced labor.

Ahijah heard whispers as people nudged each other. "There goes the Ephraimite Jeroboam, who is the new leader of the northern tribes!"

Ahijah's father said in a loud voice, "He's in charge of the forced labor gangs from the tribe of Joseph. He's a hard task-master, and makes men work. That's why the King gave him a high position. His mother was a poor widow."

A prophet also called Ahijah, who came from Shiloh, answered, "Jeroboam is a leader. We northerners need such a man."

By the time of the grape harvest, the country was excited about the plot of the prophet Ahijah and Jeroboam. The young girls were dancing among the grape vines to the music of harps and lyres, but young Ahijah was listening to the men tell how

Jeroboam escaped death by the King's soldiers and now was in Egypt sheltered by the Pharaoh Shishak. The prophet Ahijah took it upon himself to choose Jeroboam the leader of the north by meeting him alone in a field. There he tore his new garment into twelve pieces and gave Jeroboam ten pieces, saying, "Take thee ten pieces, for thus saith the Lord, the God of Israel. Behold, I will rend the kingdom out of the hand of Solomon" (I Kings 11:31).

Soon after this revolt, Solomon died and his son Rehoboam became King. Ahijah and his family were loyal to the dynasty of David.

CHAPTER XV

THE KINGDOMS OF ISRAEL AND JUDAH

AFTER SOLOMON'S DEATH the United Monarchy ended its short but glorious life of seventy-five years. It split into two kingdoms, Israel to the north, Judah to the south. The two kingdoms were separate and distinct from each other, although the boundary lines of the tribe of Benjamin, one of the two tribes of Judah, was only ten miles north of Jerusalem. Foreign powers recognized Jeroboam as King of Israel and Rehoboam as King of Judah, even taking sides as they waged war all through Rehoboam's reign. Shishak, the Pharaoh of Egypt, came to Jeroboam's aid and brought about the defeat of Judah. With Shishak before the gates of Jerusalem, Rehoboam was forced to buy him off by giving him palace and temple treasures. These included the golden shields of the king's bodyguard.

In spite of warfare between the two kingdoms, surrounding kingdoms, and invaders, Israel lasted 300 years, and Judah survived 450 years. Archaeology shows these centuries to be periods of stability and prosperity for the people as a whole. The pottery shows very little change; the foundations of the houses of the masses were substantial; a flourishing economy is evidenced by excavations at Tell Beit Misim southwest of Hebron in Judah. This was a textile center. Beth-Shemesh and Gibeon were centers of the olive oil and wine industry.

In Judah, the towns of Gibeah, Mizpah, Lachish, and Gibeon were fortified with massive casemate walls and towers. Judah, without the natural resources of Israel and located inland, had none of the luxuries of the northern kingdom which occupied the most fertile regions and benefited from commerce with Phoenicia.

From personal names stamped on jar handles, discovered by James B. Pritchard in his excavation of Gibeon, the people of this town worshipped Yahweh, God of Israel, during this period. Many of the names on the handles acknowledge the aid of Israel's god. A handle stamped with "Hananiah," means, "Yahweh has been gracious." Another stamped, "Azariah," means "Yahweh has helped.

Gibeon was one of the largest wine-producing towns. In 1960 the excavators found a wine press about three feet in diameter and one foot and ten inches deep. About four feet from this basin was a plastered vat to which was attached a shallow basin and through which the wine drained from the press into the vat. The grapes were crushed by treading on them with feet, which removed the skin and seeds, and allowed the juice to flow into the vat where it fermented. After the grape juice had turned to wine, it was dipped out of the vat into a trough which was cut into the face of the rock. The wine ran through the trough into a filtering basin. This consisted of two cylinder tanks about two feet deep and two feet in diameter, with a hole between which may have allowed the sediment to settle in one tank and run off clear into another. Nearby was a cluster of wine cellars, which suggested that the wine was funneled into large jars, then lowered into these cellars for aging and later use. The cellars were hewn out of rock, as in Isaiah's poem, 5.2:

"My beloved had a vineyard
on a very fertile hill
He digged it and cleared it of stones
and planted it with choice vines;
he built a watchtower in the midst of it
And he hewed out a wine vat in it."

Isaiah asks in 63.2:

"Why is thy apparel red
and thy garments like his that
tread in the wine press?"

These bits of poetic description paint a picture of how the wine vats were used at the time of the prophets.

The northern kingdom of Israel inherited the cosmopolitan civilization brought in by Solomon. There the king was chosen by God with a prophet as a go-between. Kings could be rejected, just as Saul, who was chosen by God through Samuel, was rejected in favor of David. This is known as the charismatic method of choosing rulers.

Jeroboam was such a ruler, having been chosen by the prophet Ahijah. Once king, he selected Shechem as the capital city of Israel. Jeroboam installed golden calves in the shrines of Shechem and Bethel. The Bible describes Jeroboam as the most wicked king in their history, because he led the people into idolatry. G. Ernest Wright interprets this to mean that Jeroboam, a religious conservative, believed God was invisibly riding upon the back of a bull, just as in the temple of Jerusalem He was thought to be invisibly enshrined upon the cherubim. At Bethel, the bulls were in full view of the worshippers, while in Jerusalem the people did not see the cherubim. The unthinking masses worshipped what they could see. This was why the Canaanite religion was so close to the worship in Israel.

Shechem was hard to defend. The next three kings of Israel used Tirzah as their capital. This is the modern mound of Tell el-Far'ah in the Jordan valley, excavated by Père de Vaux in 1947. It was a great city in the bronze ages but was destroyed in the ninth century B.C. An unfinished building identifies this site as Tirzah, the capital of Israel under Omri, before he built Samaria. The town was occupied until the Assyrians destroyed it in 722 B.C. Samaria is a most interesting Biblical site because it was built on bedrock by an Israelite king. I Kings 16:23, 24 tells us, "In the thirty and first year of Asa, King of Judah, began Omri to reign over Israel and reigned twelve years; six years reigned he in Tirzah. And he bought the hill Samaria of Shemer for two talents of silver and fortified the hill and called the name of the city which he built, after the name of Shemer the owner of the hill, Samaria."

Omri chose this hill because of its strategic position on the north-south highway, at the foot of the watershed, where he could be on the alert for any attack from Judah and yet had easy access to the civilized and sophisticated cities of Phoenicia. At the foot of the hill lay the fertile Jezreel valley with its vineyards and olive orchards, and on clear days the blue of the Mediterranean was visible.

Samaria was difficult to excavate because it was intensely occupied even during the Hellenistic and Roman periods. Archaeologists discovered the remains of Israelite walls of the ninth century on bedrock, beautifully made and faced with stones dressed flat and perfectly fitted together. The line of this finely made wall was traced around the flat summit of the hill. On the east were found remnants of some columns with capitals in the proto-Ionic style, a triangle in the middle and two spiral curves on either side. These may have been part of a monumental gateway. From hundreds of small fragments of ivory found in the excavation some ivory plaques were restored and found to be copies of Egyptian art. Hebrew and Phoenician letters carved on the backs of the plaques showed them to have been made in Sidon and Tyre. They were beautifully carved, with paste insets in cloisonné work using foil and glass. Similar ivories were found at Ras Shamra in Syria, and at Nineveh, where they may have been part of the loot captured by the Assyrian kings from Israel. Elaborate eggshell-thin pottery sherds, covered with a red slip and decorated with rings of creamy background, were found in the royal palace, and are called Samaria ware. These finds are clues to the plan of the city built by Omri on a site that had never been occupied. It is interesting to see how Omri planned a new city, because all the other Israelite cities were rebuilt on old sites and on tops of ruins.

The whole summit of the hill was the king's residence, and the magnificent wall that enclosed it was not built for military purposes. Inside was a large palace and courtyard, made of beaten earth and paved with lime plaster. I Kings 22:39 tells us that Ahab built an ivory house and many cities. He really finished the city because his father Omri died six years after he founded Samaria. Ahab fortified the city with strong casemate walls, one around the original fine wall, slightly lower and resting on a terace, and another around the base of the hill. No doubt Phoenician workshops provided all the elegant ivory carving, inlay, furniture, gold and silver utensils. A Phoenician princess, Jezebel, became his wife, and Ahab built for her a sanctuary to Baal. This helped to solidify an alliance between Israel and Phoenicia.

The farmers worshipped Yahweh as an agricultural Baal who made their lands fertile and brought rain; the rich merchants and artisans worshipped Yahweh as the Baal of bronze altars in Solomon's temple. The Yahweh of the wilderness, who had made a covenant with the people and looked after the poor and oppressed, found a champion in Elijah of Tishbeh, who came from Gilead, independent nomadic desert country of Transjordan. Elijah appeared to denounce Ahab and Jezebel for confiscating the property of Naboth who had owned a vineyard adjoining the palace which the king and queen coveted. Jezebel gave false testimony to the elders, who condoned the seizure and ordered Naboth stoned. Elijah dared to denounce the royal pair as well as the worship of Baal. People listened to him and followed him. Elijah was the first of the great prophets, who awakened the conscience of Israel and eventually lifted Judaism to its high and spiritual plane.

Elijah had to flee for his life to Beersheba because of Jezebel. Ahab was busy defending the country. Megiddo was the administrative center and military fortress of Israel. Excavations show that Ahab built thick casemate walls, staggered gates with guardrooms in huge watch towers, and more stable areas with stone mangers and upright stones with holes to which the horses were tethered. When Yigael Yadin excavated Hazor, he found casemated walls which were identical with those of Megiddo. He also discovered more stables from the ninth century which were post-Solomonic and could have belonged to Ahab. An inscription of Shalmanezer III of Assyria, who was making his first attempt to take over Syria and Palestine, reports a battle not mentioned in the Bible. Shalmanezer III claimed a great victory north of Damascus. He mentions "Ahab, the Israelite," with 2,000 chariots and 10,000 infantry, along with his allies the kings of Damascus and Hamath. Shalmanezer III evidently exaggerated his victory, because he did not take Damascus or Palestine. Ahab lost his life later trying to regain Transjordan.

Ahab's son Joram, 849-842 B.C., failed to put down the revolt of King Mesha, who commemorated the event by erecting the Moabite Stone. II Kings 3 tells how the Israelites laid siege to the

Moabite city, and Mesha, king of Moab, offered his son as a burnt offering upon the wall. The shocked and fearful Israelites returned to their own territory, which Mesha interpreted as a victory. The inscription reads, "As for Omri, King of Israel, he humbled Moab, many years, for Chemosh was angry at his land." And his son followed him and he also said, "But I have triumphed over him and his house, while Israel hath perished forever."

The Moabite Stone was first seen by a missionary, Rev. F. A. Klein, in 1868 while he was travelling east of the Dead Sea. Fortunately he made a squeeze, which is a copy made by placing soggy paper over the inscription. When this dries it retains an impression of the writing carved in stone. Eight lines were also copied. After this some Arabs broke the monument in pieces, hoping to sell it piece by piece. A French archaeologist, Clermont-Ganneau, recovered most of the pieces, and it is now in the Louvre in Paris.

In one of the buildings in the courtyard of the palace of Samaria were found a large number of ostraca, documents written on potsherds as tax receipts, for taxes paid with jars of wine or oil. A large number of these ostraca were found in one of the buildings in the courtyard of the palace of Samaria. Authorities date these ostraca to the ninth century B.C. The receipts are brief:

"In the tenth year
from Abiezer to Shemariyo
A jar of old wine."

Another reads:

"From Tetel
In the tenth year,
From Azzah to Gaddiyo.
A jar of fine oil."

All these jars of fine oil and wine could have been collected during the days of Jezebel, whose gay court was such a scandal. Evidently the Israel kings enriched their own treasuries with taxes of wine and oil, or distributed these luxuries to the nobility, who drank great quantities of wine out of bowls at their banquets, or annointed themselves with fine oil as they lay on their ivory beds. One of the disasters of that period was an earthquake at

Stone lion found at Hazor.

Courtesy Israel Exploration Society

Example of Ostraca found at Arad.

Hazor. Yigael Yadin found evidences of destruction by an earthquake at Hazor in the ninth century B.C. which must have caused great suffering and hardship among the people of Hazor.

About 100 years later in the eighth century when the herdsman from Tekoa called Amos began to prophesy, Samaria must have been just as decadent. Amos regarded the earthquake as a sign of God's displeasure. His descriptions become more vivid when we realize that all the wine and oil was really tax money belonging to the state, not for the king to use for his own pleasure. Amos 6:4, 6 reads:

"Woe to those who lie upon ivory beds. . .
Who drink wine in bowls
and annoint themselves with the finest oils."

In Chapter 3:9, Amos says: "Assemble yourselves upon the mountains of Samaria, and see the great tumults within her, and the oppressions in her midst."

According to Kathleen Kenyon, excavations show there was a marked distinction between the quarters of the rich and the poor at Tell el Far'ah or ancient Tirzah, which as we have noted, was an important town about 800 B.C. The houses of the poor were huddled together, while the houses of the rich had courtyards flanked on three sides by rooms.

Amos warned, no doubt thinking of the earthquake (Amos 9:9):

"For lo I will command,
and shake the house of Israel
among the nations . . ."

Amos still remembered the ignominious defeats heaped upon Israel by the Assyrians. A century ago, at the time of the earthquake in Hazor, the Assyrians had a new secret weapon—men on horseback—cavalry. At that time Israel and her neighbors used horses but only to pull chariots. Shalmanezer III was the human earthquake that shook Israel in about 859 B.C.

CHAPTER XVI

DOWNFALL AND EXILE

SHALMANEZER III, King of Assyria (ca. 859-824 B.C.), was a squat, muscular man in a long robe, black-bearded, with aquiline nose with coarse nostrils, thick lips, large piercing eyes, and a cruel imperious countenance. How is it possible to give such a detailed description of this king who is not even mentioned in the Bible?

In October of 1861 J. E. Taylor, a British Consul, discovered lying beside the Tigris about twenty miles south of Diyarbekir, a large stela of Shalmanezer III making a gesture of worship toward a row of divine emblems. An inscription reads that in the sixth year of his reign King Shalmanezer III left his capital city, Nineveh, on an expedition to the west. In the region of Hamath near the River Orontes, he was resisted by a strong force led by twelve kings. The inscription reads:

> "I destroyed, tore down and burned Karkara, his royal residence. He brought along to help him 1,200 chariots, 1,200 cavalrymen, 20,000 foot soldiers of Adadiri of Damascus, 700 chariots, 700 cavalrymen, 10,000 foot soldiers of Irhuleni from Hamath, 2,000 chariots, 10,000 foot soldiers of Ahab, the Israelite. . . . I slew 14,000 of their soldiers with the sword, descending upon them like Adad when he makes a rainstorm pour down. I spread their corpses everywhere, filling the entire plain

> with their widely scattered, fleeing soldiers. During the battle I made their blood flow down the Hur-pa-lu of the district. The plain was too small to let all their souls descend into the nether world, the vast field gave out when it came to bury them. With their corpses I spanned the Orontes before there was a bridge."

We know from the last chapter that Shalmanezer III was stopped and had to withdraw, but this boastful report of the Assyrian came to light through archaeology.

Shalmanezer's next Israelite victim was Jehu, King of Israel. Elijah had started a revolution among the followers of Yahweh to stamp out the corruption of the worshippers of Baal. The prophetic party was subsequently led by the prophet Elisha, who commissioned a prophet disciple to annoint the general Jehu king of Israel. This was perfectly possible under the charismatic method of selecting rulers in which the prophet, as God's representative, chose the ruler. Jehu was a bloodthirsty soldier who seized power for his own glory. First he demanded that the heads of Ahab's seventy sons be delivered to him, and the cowed authorities delivered the heads in baskets. At that time Judah and Israel were allies. When forty-two princes from Judea came on a friendly visit to Israel, Jehu slaughtered them. Next he was instrumental in the murder of Jezebel. Once seated on the throne, he oppressed the puritanical party who had given him power. He had no allies. Both Tyre and Judah were his enemies. At that time Shalmanezer III was attacking Damascus, and Jehu threw himself on the side of the Assyrians, who immortalized Jehu's humiliation on a large black stone called the Black Obelisk. This was discovered by Austen Henry Layard in December of 1846 while excavating Nimrud. It was sculptured on the four sides. In all there were twenty small bas-reliefs; above, below and between them was carved an inscription 210 lines in length. The King Shalmanezer III is twice carved in the stone, followed by his attendants. A prisoner is at his feet, while his vizier and eunuchs introduce men leading an elephant, a rhinoceros, the Bactrian two-humped camel, a wild bull, a lion, a stag, and different types of monkeys. Men carry vases and other objects of tribute on their shoulders or in their hands. The prisoner grovelling at the king's feet is Jehu. The inscription reads: "The tribute of Jehu, son of Omri, I received from him silver, gold, a golden saplu bowl, a golden vase with pointed bottom, golden tumblers, golden buckets, tin, a staff for a king, and a wooden puruthu."

For about ninety years the Assyrians did not invade the West because they were busy conquering Babylonia. During this period the two Israelite kingdoms were at war with Damascus and other kingdoms east of the Jordan. During the reigns of Joash and Jeroboam II (about 801-746 B.C.), Israel enjoyed great power and prosperity. Jeroboam conquered Damascus and the old border of David on the north in eastern Syria. In Judah, Uzziah (about 783-742 B.C.) rebuilt the smelter at Ezion-geber and called it Elath, after having subjugated Edom.

Excavations show that towns in both kingdoms were well populated. At Tell Beit Mirsim there was a weaving industry and at Gibeon and Beth-Shemesh a prosperous wine and olive oil industry. All the towns were walled, either fortified by casemate walls or sloping plastered banks at the foot. There were two types of towns: those like Samaria and Megiddo, which had palaces, official buildings, and stables for chariots; and ordinary towns of private houses, regularly laid out in blocks divided by planned streets. There was no ring of buildings around the walls, so typical of earlier towns. Bronze was still the popular metal used for ornaments like brooches, rings, earrings, seals, beads, and pendants. A few pieces of silver jewelry were discovered. Iron tools were used exclusively. Pottery was plentiful. It was utilitarian, well made but plain.

Figurines were still found in the excavations, but they had changed in style. According to Albright, the northern goddesses were musicians, fully clothed and veiled, with tambourines pressed to their breasts. The southern figurines were busts of fertility goddesses, whose huge breasts were supported by the hands as if to suckle an infant.

Prosperity and trade imported the astral cults of Babylonia; particularly popular was the myth of Tammuz and Ishtar, the Queen of Heaven.

The prophet Amos who lived in the times of Jeroboam II warned that Damascus would take Israel into exile by worshipping these "star-gods."

Hosea who followed Amos warned (Hosea 14:3), "Assyria shall not save us, we will not ride upon horses."

Finally after the Assyrians annexed the Northern Kingdom, Isaiah pleaded with the people of Judah (Isaiah 1:18):

> "Come now, let us reason together,
> Says the Lord:
> Though your sins are like scarlet,
> they shall be as white as snow;
> though they are red like crimson,
> they shall become like wool.
> If you are willing and obedient."

In 734 B.C. the Assyrian bull marched right into Palestine led by Tiglath-pileser III. From the sculptures which Austen Henry Layard discovered among the ruins of Nineveh we get his strong profile; his hair and beard are perfumed and curled with meticulous care and fall in ringlets over his shoulders and breast. His turban is shaped into a cone, trimmed with a pattern of rosettes. His robe is trimmed with precious stones and embroidered flowers, his arms are bare, and a broad embroidered girdle about his waist holds a set of daggers. All of his officers are curled and bedecked. Pul, as Tiglath-pileser III was called in the Bible, led his wild horsemen of Assur, who guided their horses by a mere pressure of a knee. After them came the charioteers, three to each heavy chariot. Then came the battalions of infantry, flying high the royal standard, the sacred disk of Assur, the divine archer, carried on two bull's heads. The troops wore conical helmets, and their leather jerkins were covered with metal scales to protect the chest and shoulders; over their close-fitting breeches was a knee-length waistcloth, and their high leather boots laced up the front. They were armed with a great wicker shield faced with metal, a bow, a short sword, and a six-foot lance. They advanced in close formation. Layard made a drawing of a relief he found at Numrud of Assyrian soldiers using a siege engine with a battering ram to attack a walled tower. Another relief shows how Tiglath-pileser terrorized his victims by hanging citizens on stakes outside the town walls, extending their hands in a gesture of surrender to bowmen advancing upon them.

Courtesy Louvre

Assyrian archer on horseback.

With this formidable army descending upon them, the kings of Damascus and Tyre as well as Israel's king Menahem all paid Tiglath-pileser tribute. Menahem gave the Assyrian a thousand talents of silver which he raised by taxing all the wealthy men fifty shekels of silver (II Kings 15:20), "So the king of Assyria turned back and did not stay in the land."

The story of Tiglath-pileser comes from an inscription published by Rawlinson. "As for Menahem I overwhelmed him like a snowstorm and he . . . fled like a bird, alone, and bowed to my feet. I returned him to his place and imposed tribute upon him to wit: gold, silver, linen garments with multicolored trimmings . . . I received from him Israel . . . all its inhabitants and their possessions I led to Assyria. They overthrew their king Pekah and I placed Hoshea as king over them. I received from them 10 talents of gold, 1,000 talents of silver as their tribute and brought them to Assyria."

To continue with the Biblical account of the story: Menahem died and his son was murdered by a General Pekah, who seized power and entered the palace with a body of fifty Gileadites. Pekah allied himself with Damascus, the Phoenician seaports of Sidon and Tyre, some Philistine towns and an Arab queen by the name of Shamsi, against the Assyrians. The Hittites in north Syria, part of Philistia, Amon, Moab, Edom, and Judah refused to join the alliance. Pekah with his ally, Damascus, declared war on these recalcitrant states and marched into Judah. They helped Edom capture the copper refinery and seaport of Elath, and planned to annex Judah and put one of their own men on the throne. Jerusalem was in a state of panic. The king, Ahaz, appealed to Tiglath-pileser for help by sending him silver and gold from the Temple and palace treasures. In the meantime he prepared for the siege of Pekah and Damascus. While inspecting the water supply of the city at the end of the conduit of the upper pool he was confronted by the prophet Isaiah, who said, "Keep calm and be quiet; fear not, neither let thy heart be faint. Judah will not be overcome by Damascus and Pekah. If ye will not have faith, surely ye shall not be established" (Isaiah 7:9, 18). The prophet was so sure there was no danger of attack, he asked the king, "Ask thee a sign of the Lord thy God; ask it either in the depth, or in the height above." Ahaz said, "I will not ask, neither will I try the Lord." Then Isaiah made his famous prophecy of a messiah from the house of David whom he expected in his own lifetime. "Behold the young woman shall conceive and bear a son, and shall call his name Immanuel (God is with us). Before the boy is three years old, the invaders will have departed from Judah. The land will be laid waste by Egypt and Assyria. The riches of Damascus and the spoil of Samaria shall be carried away before the king of Assyria. Evil days will come upon Judah. But a remnant will return to the simple life of old and an ideal king will reign with everlasting peace and justice." So the prophet planted hope and faith not only in the hearts of people of his generation, but ever since people hope with Isaiah the time will come (Isaiah 2:4):

"And they shall beat their swords into plowshares,
And their spears into pruning-hooks;
Nation shall not lift up sword against nation,
Neither shall they learn war any more."

The Assyrian army swept over Israel and took Gilead and north eastern Galilee. The whole population was deported, and their land was taken over by other exiles whom the Assyrians brought in. Damascus did not fall so easily. Tiglath-pileser besieged it for two years. When the city surrendered he killed the king and deported the population. Samaria was still intact. Pekah was assassinated by Hoshea, who became king. Hoshea stopped paying tribute, and Shalmanezer captured Hoshea and imprisoned him. But Samaria held out against him, and Shalmanezer died before the city fell. Sargon II finished Israel.

Sargon's palace at Khorsabad, which we mentioned in Chapter III, was discovered by Paul Emile Botta in 1843. This site, which over a period of ten years of excavations, revealed thirty-one courts, two hundred and nine rooms, a ziggurat, a temple, all built on a terrace from forty-six to fifty feet high. From this temple the great works of Asyrian art were transported to the Louvre in Paris. They were great sculptors, these Assyrian artists, especially the bas-reliefs of animals. Their horses are full of grace and movement, as the king Ashurbanipal rides them to the chase. The reliefs are cruel, showing animals pierced by arrows, others bitten by hounds and pulled down. Sargon II hunted down people as he

Courtesy Louvre

Sargon II and his viziers.

did animals. On the walls of his palace he wrote: "I besieged and conquered Samaria, led away as booty 27,290 inhabitants of it. I formed, from among them, a contingent of fifty chariots, and made the remaining inhabitants assume their social positions. I installed over them an officer of mine and imposed upon them the tribute of the former king. The town I rebuilt better than it was before and settled therein people from countries which I myself had conquered."

Excavations at Samaria show the complete destruction of the royal palace at Samaria.

In 705 B.C. Sennacherib was leading the Assyrians down the coast of Syria and Palestine taking Sidon, Acco, Ashkelon, and defeated the Egyptians in the plain of Elketah. Ammon, Edom, and Moab made peace; only Judah resisted.

On a pillar in his palace at Nineveh, Sennacherib's scribes wrote:

> "As to Hezekiah the Judean, he did not submit to my yoke. I laid siege to 46 of his strong cities, walled forts and to countless small villages in their vicinity and conquered them by means of well stamped earth ramps and battering rams brought thus near to the walls combined with the attack by foot soldiers using mines, breeches, as well as sapper work. I drove out of them 200,150 people; young, old, male and female, horses, mules, donkeys, camels, big and small cattle beyond counting, and considered them booty. Himself I made a prisoner in Jerusalem his royal residence like a bird in a cage. I surrounded him with earth work in order to molest those who were leaving his city's gate. His towns which I had plundered, I took away from his country and gave them over to Mitinti, king of Ashdod, Padi, king of Ekron, and Sillibel, king of Gaza. Thus I reduced his country, but I still increased the tribute . . . to be delivered annually."

Sennacherib did not capture Jerusalem. He was so proud of his conquest of Lachish that a large picture of the event was carved in low relief and installed in his palace at Nineveh. There A. H. Layard found it. The relief shows both the battle and the surrender. Judean defenders are slinging stones, shooting bows and arrows, and throwing down firebrands from the towers above the city wall upon the wooden siege engines. Soldiers are digging trenches under the foundations of the walls. Assyrian bowmen, spearmen and slingers are covering the diggers. Earthen ramps have been erected up the slopes against the outer wall, and large wheeled wagons have been pushed up the ramps to the walls. Sennacherib is enthroned, his chariot and elaborate tent beside him. In front is the inscription: "Sennacherib, king of the world, king of the land of Asshur, on the nimedu chair, and the booty of the city of Lachish has before him passed." The elders of the city in their long white robes bow before the king, and behind them a long line of Judean men and women guarded by Assyrian soldiers, with carts and valuables as though prepared for a long journey.

Lachish was one of the largest cities of Palestine and was fortified by the pass leading up to Hebron. Evidence of this destruction was found in the debris of the lower roadway: a crest of a bronze helmet identical with those shown in the relief, fragments of Assyrian armor and some weapons.

In the meantime Hezekiah in Jerusalem had prepared for the siege when he "stopped the upper spring of the waters of Gihon and brought them straight down on the west side of the city

Courtesy Louvre

An Israelite family is taken prisoner by the Assyrians.

of David" (II Kings 20:20 and II Chronicles 32:30). This is the tunnel Edward Robinson dragged himself through in the nineteenth century. In 1880 an inscription was discovered on the wall which when translated really proved this to be Hezekiah's tunnel. One hot summer day a native boy crawled into the tunnel to cool off. He kept crawling through the tunnel until he reached the spring. There he accidentally fell into the water. As he got up he noticed an inscription on the wall. He told his schoolmaster, a Herr Conrad Schick, about the inscription. Herr Shick crawled through the tunnel after the boy to the spot of the inscription and recognized it as written in ancient Hebrew. Herr Schick reported this discovery to scholars, among them Professor A. H. Sayce, who copied it by candle light, made a squeeze of it, and had casts made from the squeeze. The encrustation which had filled in the letters was removed by a treatment of dilute hydrochloric acid. The first part of the inscription was missing, but this is what the scholars translated:

> "And this was the way in which it was cut through: While . . . were still . . . picks, each man toward his fellow, and while there were three cubits to be cut through, there was heard the voice of a man calling to his fellow, for there was an overlap in the rock on the right and on the left. And when the tunnel was driven through, the quarrymen hewed the rock, each man toward his fellow, pick against pick; and the water flowed from the spring toward the reservoir for 1,200 cubits, and the rock above the heads of the quarrymen was 100 cubits."

Modern excavators found the tunnel to be 1,749 feet long with an average height of five feet eleven inches. The tunnel is S-shaped and a puzzle to modern engineers, because it would have been easier to dig it in a straight line.

The tunnel is a remarkable engineering accomplishment, and did provide a safe supply of water which enabled the city of Jerusalem to withstand the Assyrian siege.

The Siloam inscription along with the Gezer calendar is one of the oldest Hebrew inscriptions. This script may be the way Isaiah wrote and spelled. The ostraca from Samaria toward 800 B.C. could be the writing of Amos.

For more than a century after the fall of Samaria, the kingdom of Judah survived, subject to the overlordship of Assyria. Hezekiah's son Manasseh (692-38) was completely submissive as a vassal of Assyria. He not only paid his tribute regularly, but provided Judean soldiers for the Assyrian expeditionary force in Egypt. The Assyrian cult of the heavenly constellations supplanted the law of Moses; an image of Ishtar, the Assyrian queen of heaven, was erected in the Temple, and in the valley of Hinnon west and southwest of Jerusalem, children were passed through fire, and Manasseh offered his own son to the fire god.

Manasseh was succeeded by his son Amon, who was murdered. When the young Josiah followed Amon to the throne of Judah, the prophets Nahum and Zepaniah predicted Nineveh's downfall. Their predictions were based on actual happenings, for the Assyrians were on the run in the north from the horse-riding Scythians who came from the steppes of Russia. The Assyrians were menaced by Babylonia in the south. Booty was plentiful in Assyria. The Scythians were bronze workers, and are given credit for designing the posture of horses in the flying gallop used in art. This unnatural posture is typical of Assyrian bas-reliefs. The Scythians invaded the coasts of Syria and Palestine on their way to Egypt but by-passed Palestine. In the meantime, according to the Babylonian Chronicle, Nabopolassar of Akkad (or Babylonia) pitched camp against Assyria, and the king of Assyria fled, "many prisoners of the city beyond counting, they carried away. The city they turned into ruin-hills and heaps of debris." Nineveh fell in 612 B.C., and the Assyrian empire was taken over by Babylonia.

The reign of Manasseh was long and back-sliding, but at least the country was at peace. It is thought by some authorities the code of Deuteronomy was written at this time. This book of the law contains the humanitarian spirit of prophets like Micah who wrote (Micah 6:8):

> "What does the Lord require of thee,
> But to do justice and love mercy
> and to walk humbly with thy God?"

Josiah was a small boy when he became king, and no doubt was influenced by those men in Judah who were turning back to the Mosaic tradition. When he was eighteen he ordered the temple repaired. A new book of the law was found in one of the rooms. After the king read the law he realized how far the nation had strayed from the law of Moses. Still, he was not sure this was the genuine law of Moses, so he submitted it to an aged prophetess named Huldah for verification. She accepted this code as that of Moses. As a consequence Josiah undertook a great religious reform.

Josiah's reform is particularly interesting, since archaeology has brought to light a letter from the first half of the seventh century B.C. According to Frank Moore Cross, Jr. in his Epigraphic Notes on Hebrew Documents of the eighth to sixth century B.C., this letter was written a full generation before the Lachish letters which we discuss later on. This letter written on papyrus palimpsest came from Murabba'at in the Judean wilderness. Evidently Josiah had attempted to revive the kingdom of David by conquest, and established a coastal fort in the vicinity of Megiddo. Josiah died in a battle with the Egyptian Pharaoh Necho II at Megiddo in 609 B.C.

This letter was written in a cursive script and was the petition of a poor man to Hashaiah, the military commander of a fortress. The man's garment has been seized for an alleged non-fulfillment of an obligation. He claims this an injustice and asks that his garment be returned. The man is in the right (Deuteronomy 24:10-13):

> "When you make your neighbor a loan of any sort, you shall not go into his house to fetch his pledge. You shall stand outside and the man to whom you make the loan shall bring the pledge out to you. And if he is a poor man you shall not sleep in his pledge. When the sun goes down you shall restore to him the pledge that he may sleep in his cloak and bless you."

The letter is as follows:

> "Let the lord the commander hear the word of his servant. As for thy servant . . . was harvesting in Hasar'Asam

and thy servant harvested and took measure and stored grain according to regular practise. Before Sabbath when thy servant had measured his harvest—Hashaiah the son of Shobay came and took the garment of thy servant. When I had measured this harvest of mine in the regular way, he took the garment of thy servant, and all my brethren will testify for me, those who were harvesting with me in the heat of the sun. . . . Truly I am innocent of any guilt. Pray return my garment. And if not, it is still incumbent on the commander to return the garment to thy servant. So let him grant him mercy thy servant, but do not drive him away."

Dr. Cross observed that the peasant might have owed the military a share of his crop which he failed to deliver. No doubt he was a small farmer or sharecropper working near Hasar'Asam. Since the petitioner was right according to Israelite law in demanding the return of his garment, if the commander was able to read the letter and a just man, he returned the garment.

During this period the prophet Jeremiah was a young man who allied himself with the reformers. He wrote (Jeremiah 3:12):

"Return thou backsliding Israel,
Saith the Lord:
I will not frown upon you;
For I am merciful, saith the Lord,
I will not bear grudge forever,
Only acknowledge thine iniquity,

That thou hast transgressed against the Lord thy God."

After Josiah's death his son Jehoiachin favored a policy of friendship with Egypt. Jeremiah disagreed and advised the king to be loyal to Babylon. Jehoiachin took Jeremiah's advice and maintained his allegiance to Babylon for three years. Abruptly he broke away.

A letter written in Aramaic found at Saqqara in Egypt in 1942 and published by John Bright throws some light on why the Judean king revolted. First this Aramaic papyrus is important because it shows that Aramaic script was at that time the international diplomatic language instead of cuneiform. Aramaic was the official language of the Persian Empire as early as 700 B.C. It was also the official language in the time of Hezekiah, when he paid tribute to Sennacherib. The scribe tells the Assyrian general (II Kings 18:26): "Speak I pray thee to thy servants in the Aramean language; for we understand it."

The Aramaic letter is from a Palestine king asking the pharaoh for help against Babylon which, according to a report, had been defeated by the Egyptians. This defeat supposedly came in about 601 B.C. and caused the King of Judah to hope falsely that an alliance with Egypt would bring freedom from Babylon. The Babylonians did not brag about themselves like the Assyrians, but recorded the chief events of each year on tablets. In 1956 D. J. Wiseman of the British Museum announced the discovery of four more tablets of the Chronicle. For the first time outside the Bible, Nebuchadnezzar's capture of Jerusalem is described from 598-597, as well as the above information and other events between 626 and 594 B.C. The new fragments of the Chronicle tell us that Nebuchadnezzar in the seventh year of his reign marched his army into the land of Khatti (Syria and Palestine) and besieged Jerusalem. He captured the city on the second day of the twelfth month of his seventh year, which was mid-March 597 B.C., and took the king prisoner.

This would correspond with the last king of Judah (597-587), Zedekiah, who came to the throne after his brother Jehoiachin, whom Nebuchadnezzar had deported to Babylon, along with the queen mother, his harem, the nobility, the army, as well as 1,000 craftsmen and their families. Some of the sacred vessels and treasures from the Temple were carried off to Babylon as booty. This was Nebuchadnezzar's first attack on Jerusalem. He put Zedekiah on the throne under an oath to serve the King of Babylon.

There was a revolutionary faction which still hoped to get help from Egypt. Isaiah had aptly described Egypt (Isaiah 36:6) as a bruised reed. "Whereon if a man lean on it, it will go into his hand and pierce it; so is Pharaoh King of Egypt to all that trust on him." This Egyptian faction appealed to women who were worshipping Ishtar, the Babylonian goddess of love, and her son Tammuz, and the men who worshipped the sun-god and sacred animals of Egypt. In 594 B.C. embassies from Ammon, Moab, Tyre, and Sidon tried to induce Zedekiah to join them in a coalition against Babylon. Reports came from exiles in Babylon predicting the collapse of the Babylonian power, and false prophets were lulling the people to sleep with the weakness of Babylon.

Jeremiah knew this was nothing but wishful thinking. He wrote letters to the exiles advising them to prepare to stay in Babylon, build houses, make homes for themselves, and pray for the welfare of Babylon, until God in His own time should lead them back. He came into the market place with a yoke around his neck as a symbol of Babylon's continued power. Hananiah of Gibeon, a false prophet from the opposition, broke the yoke in front of all the people. As a result, King Zedekiah sided with Egypt, and Babylon put an end to Jerusalem.

The people in the prosperous cities outside of Jerusalem hated Jeremiah, because he prophesied doom unless they returned to the true worship of God. Some time previously, an official called Pashhur struck Jeremiah and put him in stocks. Of this he wrote pathetically (Jeremiah 20:7):

> "O Lord Thou hast enticed me, and I was enticed,
> Thou hast overcome me, and hast prevailed:
> I am become a laughing stock all the day,
> Everyone mocketh me."

In verse 11 of the same chapter he takes heart:

> "But the Lord is with me as a mighty warrior;
> Therefore my persecutors shall stumble and they
> shall not prevail."

Archaeology does not have much evidence of Judah's last century. Tell Beit Mirsim, an important textile center, was destroyed by the Babylonians and never occupied again. Beth Shemesh and Gibeon ceased to exist at that time. Gibeon was destroyed and limestone blocks from the city wall thrown into the underground pool to stop up the supply of water.

Jerusalem was completely sacked and destroyed. King Zedekiah fled to Jericho. He was captured and made to witness the slaughter of his sons and members of the nobility by the Babylonians; then his eyes were put out and he was taken in chains to Babylon. The population was taken captive to Babylon.

In the meantime Jeremiah had been put into a dungeon. The king held a secret meeting with the prophet, who pleaded with the King to surrender. The war party persisted in fighting Babylon and Jeremiah remained in prison.

The Babylonians had no intention of annihilating the Jewish nation. So on the very day Jerusalem was destroyed, Nebuzaradan, the Babylonian general, set up an autonomous Jewish group at Mizpah with Gedaliah as governor. Nebuchadnezzar rewarded Jeremiah with a pension for his loyalty. Only the poor people remained in Judah. The rich, the skilled, the noble, had been deported. These details we know from the Bible.

The last days of the Kingdom of Judah have come from eighteen pieces of broken pottery found in the guard room of Lachish when it was excavated by James L. Starkey in 1935. Jeremiah listed Lachish and Azekah together with Jerusalem among the strongholds of Judah, "for these fenced cities remained of the cities of Judah" (Jeremiah 34:7).

The ashes that covered these sherds are remains of the final destruction of Lachish. It was never occupied again as a town, though it later served as an administrative center. Out of these ashes the excavators salvaged letters written in good Biblical Hebrew with iron-carbon ink on pieces of pottery. Professor H. Torczyner translated them and interpreted them in this way:

These letters are part of a correspondence between Ya'ush, the commander of Lachish, and Hosha'yahu, the commander of a fortified post.

Hosha'yahu writes the commander of Lachish, "And let my lord know that we are watching for the signals of Lachish, according to all the indications which my lord hath given, for we cannot see Azekah." If this was the time Babylon was attacking Jerusalem and the rest of the Judean cities, this might mean that Azekah mentioned by Jeremiah had already fallen. No doubt the signals were made by fire or smoke. We get a picture of an outpost on a hill, serving as a communication center for the Judean army. This seems to be the only one written before Lachish fell.

The others may have been written earlier, and as Torczyner

points out, suggest a court-martial of Hosha'yahu, the writer of the letters. A room at the gate of the city is traditionally the place where courts of justice are held in Near Eastern countries. Through all the intelligible letters Hosha'yahu seems to be trying to excuse himself, and deny he has committed a crime by reading some confidential letters he was entrusted to forward. Instead he read the letters and informed the king or his officers that the prophet Uriah had fled to Egypt.

Uriah was a prophet who also prophesied doom like Jeremiah just before the first captivity by Babylon. The king sentenced him to death, but he escaped into Egypt. Evidently Uriah was betrayed because in Jeremiah 26:23 the king sent Commander Elnathan after Uriah into Egypt and he was brought back to Jerusalem and killed.

Ya'ush might have belonged to the party of Jeremiah who favored submission to Babylon and accused Hosha'yahu of betrayal.

Whether or not this is an exact interpretation of the letters, they bring to life the language, names, and details of conditions when Jeremiah lived and wrote.

In letter III, which is the longest, Hosha'yahu defends himself by saying he has not called in a scribe to read for him. Evidently a scribe wrote the letters.

"Thy servant Hosha'yahu hath sent to inform my lord Ya'ush: May Yahweh cause my lord to hear tidings of peace! And now thou hast sent a letter, but my lord did not enlighten thy servant concerning the letter which thou didst send to thy servant yesterday evening, though the heart of thy servant hath been sick since thou didst write to thy servant. And as for what my lord said, 'Dost thou not understand?—call a scribe!' as Yahweh liveth no one hath ever undertaken to call a scribe for me; and as for any scribe who might have come to me, truly, I did not call him nor would I give anything at all for him!

"And it hath been reported to thy servant, saying, 'The commander of the host, Coniah son of Elnathan, hath come down in order to go into Egypt; and unto Hodadiah son of Ahijah hath he sent to obtain . . . from him.' "

Lachish was violently destroyed by the Babylonians. In the gateway eight feet of burnt debris separated the floors of this period from those above it. The palace citadel was completely ruined. Nearby were some shops, left as the inhabitants fled leaving large storage jars used for grain and a weaving establishment. Outside the city were the remains of 2,000 bodies thrown into an old tomb, which the excavator, J. L. Starkey, surmised was the way the Babylonians cleaned up the city after the savage slaughter. Three skulls have been found that were trephined. The surgery was crude, a square of skull bone had been removed by saw cuts. Two of the victims did not survive. A third person in which the hole had been made by scraping lived long enough for the bone to heal; it was an old operation and not the immediate cause of death. Trephining may have been used by Israelite surgeons to treat battle casualties.

The devastations were as complete as the descriptions in the Book of Lamentations. Jeremiah weeps (Lamentations 1:1):

> "How doth the city sit solitary;
> that was full of people! How is she become as a widow!
> She that was great among the nations, and the princess
> among the provinces, how is she become a tributary!"

The refugees who had gone to Mizpah suffered from the Ammonite king, who caused the murder of their governor, Gedaliah, because he wanted to take over Judah himself.

These poverty-stricken Jews emigrated to the delta in Egypt, and dragged along Jeremiah into involuntary exile. Jeremiah found Jewish communities in both lower and upper Egypt. Some had been brought there as slaves, others had settled as merchants since the time of Solomon and his trade in horses; others were mercenaries in the Egyptian army. These Jews clung to their nationality, but practiced the same religion they knew in the rural districts of Judea. Jeremiah scolded them for their worship of the "Queen of Heaven." But Jeremiah never lost his faith in God (Jeremiah 24:7):

> "I will give them a heart to know me,
> That I am the Lord;
> And they shall be my people,
> And I will be their God,
> For they shall return to me, with their whole heart."

CHAPTER XVII
THE WORLD OF THE DISPERSION AND RETURN

THE LITERATE WORLD had expanded by the middle of the first millennium B.C. to five times the known area of Ancient Egypt and Mesopotamia in the Bronze Age. By 500 B.C. there were civilized communities from Spain on the Atlantic to the Jaxartes River in central Asia and the Ganges in India, and from southern Arabia to the north coasts of the Mediterranean and the Black Sea. Persian rule extended over Egypt, Palestine, Syria, Asia Minor, the former Assyrian and Babylonian empires to Gandara in India. The Phoenicians had colonized Spain and North Africa with farmers, fishermen and traders, because there was no room for expansion on the narrow coastal plain of Syria. The Etruscans had settled on the western coasts and central plains of Italy, conquering, for a time, the Romans. By 500 B.C. the Romans overthrew this monarchy and became a republic.

With the wine and olive oil industries destroyed in Palestine and Egypt reduced to an agricultural country, Greece emerged as the world supplier of wine, olive oil, pottery, and silver. The prosperous Greeks occupied all the islands of the Aegean, the coasts of the Black Sea, southern Italy and Campania to Marseilles, a seaport in western Europe. This was the period of the greatest Greek art.

The sprawling Assyrian and Babylonian empires, in spite of their boasts of tearing and burning down palaces, spreading corpses everywhere, and deporting mass populations to different parts of the empire, did unify and bring into contact all kinds of cultures. There was communication and pooling of knowledge. The Assyrians and Persians unintentionally promoted human communication through their systems of roads.

"The Royal Road" of the Persians was equipped with inns and relays of horses for the use of official messengers. The prime purpose of this road was to collect tribute. Besides tax and tribute collectors, trade caravans, troops and travelers on these roads explored this new world. Herodotus, the Greek historian, traveled to Babylon. Egyptian physicians traveled to Persia, and the Babylonian scientists must have come in contact with the Greeks, who admit they took their science from the Babylonians and Egypt as well as their art and architecture.

The Israelites had been deported to all parts of Mesopotamia, but the Judeans, who were deported to Babylon, we now call Jews. The Israelites known as the "ten lost Tribes," were probably assimilated in the cosmopolitan population of the Empire. As individuals they may have traveled to Jewish centers and identified themselves with the Jewish population. The exile in Babylonia had made the Jews conscious of their religious uniqueness which made them different from other peoples. Now the Mosaic laws, the sabbath, and festival celebrations held them together. Among them was Ezekiel, a great prophet and teacher, who had been deported in the first exile. His prophecy in the form of visions drew up a plan for the rebuilding of the Temple and a reorganization of the Mosaic law for the re-establishment of Israel. He preached that religion was a matter for the individual person, who was rewarded or punished for his own deeds, not for those of another.

Lofty moral and religious ideas were being taught in other parts of the world at this time. Gautama Buddha attained enlightenment in India around 500 B.C. Moral virtues, obedience to parents, respect for all living creatures, and truthfulness were Buddha's teaching. From Buddhism came monasticism, which centuries later played an important part in Christianity. In the sixth century Lao-tse and Confucius in China taught a rational morality. In Greece the first natural philosophers, Thales (625-540) and Anaximander (600-530) of Miletus, had given a name to the order of nature, "Cosmos." Thales, when asked what was difficult, answered, "To know thyself." What is easy? He said, "To give advice." What is God? He answered, "That which has neither beginning nor end." How to live most virtuously? "If we never do ourselves what we blame in others."

Ideas as well as trade and skills were diffused throughout this expanded world, in which people now communicated with each other by means of travel. As time went on, the Jews in Babylon prospered, along with Babylon which was known as "the city of merchants." Some of the Jews were quite influential in court circles and persuaded Evil-Merodach, the son of Nebuchadnezzar, to release the Jewish king Jehoiachin from prison and accord him royal honors. Then the country was conquered by the Medes, and the Medes were displaced by Cyrus the Persian. Cyrus made a written declaration granting permission to the Jews to return to Jerusalem and rebuild the Temple of the God of heaven.

Cyrus was a Zoroastrian, the official religion of the Achaemedian or Persian rulers who followed him. Some concepts found in both the Old and New Testaments stem directly from Zoroastrianism, which is not mentioned anywhere in the Bible.

Zoroaster, also called Zarathustra, the founder of this religion, is said to have been born in Northern Iran about the seventh century B.C. At fifteen years of age he dedicated himself to a religious life, and when he was thirty he is believed to have had a direct call into the presence of Ahura Mazda to receive his blessings and instructions for founding this religion. From this time Zoroaster conferred with Ahura Mazda, and preached a universal, progressive religion among the agricultural communities in Persia. He converted the King Vistapa and his court, including his counselor whose daughter Zoroaster married. The sacred book of this religion is called Avesta, meaning knowledge. He lived to the age of seventy-seven and was killed by barbarian invaders. The tradition of his life is filled with stories of miracles and of divine prophecies of his birth and deeds. His teaching is lofty and spiritual, based on the principle of the fight between good and evil. Ahura Mazda is symbolic of light and good. Ahriman is darkness or evil, like Satan of the Bible. Associated with Ahura Mazda are a number of divine personalities who play the same part as angels in the Bible. Fire is holy, and sacred fire altars were maintained in honor of Ahura Mazda. The history of the world is the incessant struggle between the two principles of good and evil. The Mazdaists believed in the immortality of the soul which crossed a bridge of judgment after death. If a person had led a good life, he went to the "Abode of Hymns." If he was evil he went to hell with the druj, who were demons and ghouls. At the end of time a messiah was to appear, named Saoshyant the son of Zoroaster, and stand at the side of Zoroaster, who would preside over the resurrection of the dead. A flood of molten metal would cover the earth, bringing about the last judgment. All the evil people, including Ahriman, would be destroyed, the good would be saved, and this would mark the ultimate triumph of good over evil.

Orthodox Zoroastrians exposed their dead to vultures, rather than burying them, for fear of contaminating the sacred principles of fire, earth, and water by contact with dead bodies. This religion still survives in India and Pakistan among a small minority of people called Parsis.

The Jews benefited from this tolerant religion when Cyrus allowed them to return to Jerusalem and rebuild the Temple.

An unknown poet called the Deutero-Isaiah had a great influence on the new community in Jerusalem, especially the common people. He not only sang of one transcendent God whose truth is incompatible with any other; he also taught that Israel had been redeemed to be the teacher of mankind, a light to all nations, the one who will spread God's Torah to all men. He emphasized humility and meekness in the presence of tormentors, and steadfast faith in God (Isaiah 53:7-8, 10-12):

> "He was oppressed and he was afflicted,
> yet he opened not his mouth . . .
> By oppression and judgment he was taken away . . .
> Yet it was the will of the Lord to bruise him . . .
> because he poured out his soul to death,
> and was numbered with the transgressors;
> yet he bore the sin of many,
> and made intercession for the transgressors."

Many Jews remained in Babylonia. The new Judean community established in Palestine during the sixth and fifth centuries occupied a small area of twenty-five miles which extended north from Jerusalem only a few miles, and south to Beth-zur. By 440 B.C. the population was about 50,000 according to Nehemiah (Nehemiah 7:66). They were surrounded by hostile neighbors. The newcomers looked down upon those who had remained in Palestine as being of mixed blood because they had intermarried. The inhabitants resented the claims of the returned refugees that they were the only true followers of the Jewish faith. When Nehemiah drove out Manasseh, the grandson of the High Priest Eliashib because he had intermarried with those of mixed race, Sanballat, governor of Samaria, built a temple for him on Mount Gerizim as a rival to the temple in Jerusalem. This sect was known as Samaritans. There began a conflict of religious centers which has continued to modern times.

Nehemiah, cup bearer to the Persian king, was governor of Judea. He rebuilt the walls of Jerusalem and cooperated with Ezra, a priest well versed in the Mosaic Torah. Conditions for the early settlers in Palestine had been very hard, with crop failures, unfriendly Samaritans, Amorites, and invading Arabs. Poor debt-ridden farmers had sold themselves into slavery. The upper classes intermarried with the idolators. Injustice and harshness was rampant. There was a body of men headed by the prophet Malachi who gave themselves up to fasting and self-abnegation, and questioned whether it was profitable to serve God. Malachi saw the solution in a day of judgment as a purifying act, with Elijah coming down from heaven.

Ezra, horrified at conditions, read sections of the Torah to the assembled people on the first of Tishri, 445 B.C. People fasted and bound themselves to observe the laws of the Torah. It was stipulated that no marriages should be contracted with surrounding nations. The land should lie fallow and all debts paid every seventh year. Dues for the upkeep of the Temple and priests should be regularly paid, and the Sabbath honored by excluding all business transactions, even with non-Jewish traders.

The resettlement of Judah was a slow process, and the population did not approximate that of the country before the destruction by Nebuchadnezzar until the third century B.C. Archaeologists have found no trace of the temple rebuilt by Zerubbabel or the walls built by Nehemiah. Buildings connected with the administration by the Babylonians and Persians have been excavated.

A Persian palace was found at the top of the mound of Lachish, from the late fifth or early fourth century B.C. This introduced a new type of architecture into Palestine. It was built around a large courtyard like Mesopotamian buildings, and some of the rooms had doors and ceilings covered by barrel vaults. This was the same type of construction used later on by the Romans in the Near East. This palace was built a century after Lachish was destroyed, and was not the administrative center of Judah, but of Idumaea, the country of the semi-nomadic Edomites who had taken over territory in Palestine. There were no private houses of a town around the palace.

Sites on the Mediterranean coast show trade with Greece and South Arabia. Beautiful Greek vases and lamps have been found in homes of the well-to-do along the coast. Along the south coastland of Palestine small square limestone incense altars with four short legs and a shallow trough on top were found. The sides were decorated with palm trees, camels, wild goats, wild donkeys, and antelopes. Similar altars have been found in South Arabia, which was the supplier of spices and incense to the Mediterranean. Caravan stations dotted a 1,500-mile route from South Arabia to the Mediterranean. Beautiful silver vessels were discovered at Gezer and Tell el-Farah in southern Palestine, which came from Syria and were typical of the work of the whole Persian Empire.

The most important invention of this period was coinage. This originated in Lydia in western Asia Minor on the Aegean Sea and spread rapidly through Asia and among the Greeks. Ancient money values were based on the Sumerian metric standards, of dividing a circle into three hundred and sixty degrees, of the day into twenty-four hours, an hour into sixty minutes, a foot into twelve inches, a pound as it survives in our troy weight of twelve ounces. The system is based on the numbers six or twelve and their multiple sixty. The weights in the ancient Near East also increased by sixties. Their ancient money values were based on these weights. The Hebrew maneh was approximately a pound or the equivalent of sixty shekels. This brought commerce within the sphere of the small merchant or workman.

Before coinage all precious metal like gold and silver came in ingots and had to be weighed. A man would have to wait perhaps days to get his wages. A shekel is a quarter of an ounce, and sixty shekels had to be carefully weighed. Now he received a coin worth that much. The Persian authorities allowed the high priests of Judah to strike their own coinage and levy their own temple taxes. Silver coins were struck in imitation of Greek drachmas with the Hebrew or Aramaic inscription Yehud, or Judah. Jar stamps of this period and early Hellenistic times leave the imprint Yehud or Yerushalem.

Archaeological excavations of a Jewish colony in Babylonia were made by an American expedition from the University of Pennsylvania between 1889 and 1900, and again in 1948 by the University of Chicago and the University Museum of Philadelphia, at Nippur southeast of Babylon. Seven hundred tablets of the fifth century B.C. were discovered, which were the records of a large Babylonian firm of bankers and brokers. There were many Hebrew names in the documents, showing that a great number of exiles had taken Jeremiah's advice and permanently settled in the district. Many inscribed Hebrew bowls indicate that a colony of Jews lived in Nippur for centuries. There was also a large colony of Jews in Babylonia who did not return to Jerusalem. This was the beginning of the eastern seat of Jewry which in succeeding centuries had far-reaching influences which shaped Jewish life and strengthened Jewish resistance. These people supplied the funds for Ezra's return with a colony of repatriots, took pride in the restored temple and ever after contributed to its maintenance.

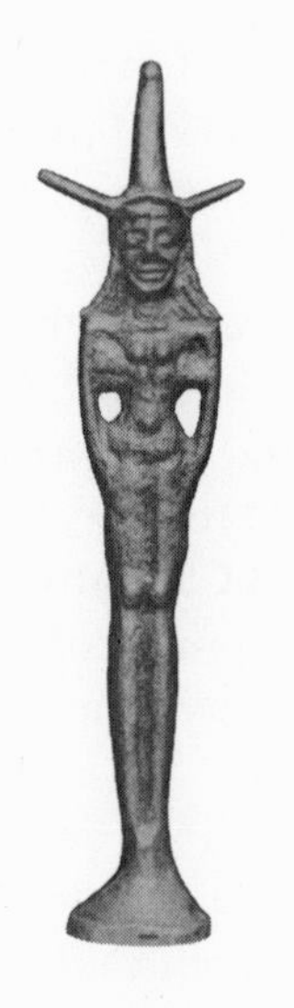

CHAPTER XVIII

HELLENISM, ITS LIFE AND TIMES

330 B.C. to 63 B.C.

IN THE YEAR 334 B.C. Alexander the Great crossed the Hellespont and conquered Asia Minor. After defeating Darius III of Persia in the battle of Issus, he mopped up Tyre, Gaza, and went down into Egypt where he founded the city of Alexandria in the Delta. The Jews helped him in Egypt, and he promised them equal rights with the Greeks in the new city of Alexandria. In the spring he headed for the heart of the Persian Empire, and passed through Palestine and Syria, where the Jews accepted a change of masters. The Samaritans objected to Alexander's governor, Andromachus. They burned him alive in oil. Alexander was so incensed he punished them very severely, and the city of Samaria was compelled to admit Macedonian settlers.

On thousand six hundred twenty-nine years later, in December of the year 1963, some Bedouins whom a drought had driven north were guarding their flocks at Mugharet Abu Sinjeh in the Wadi Dalihj. The sharp-eyed Bedouins spotted some caves high up on the mountain. Caves meant only one thing to Bedouins, scrolls! And scrolls meant money. The cave was 1,500 feet above the Jordan and 325 feet above sea level. The Bedouins eventually reported the caves to archaeologists (after selling their own finds). The excavators went up by donkey and constructed terraces for their tents to escape flash floods. The cave was 65 meters deep, full of bats and guano. The diggers were choked by clouds of dust. In a remote recess of a deep passageway they found fourth-century Palestine pottery and early Roman pottery. There they saw the skeletons—male, female, young, and old—200 or 300 of them!

They found two gold rings and some seals with Persian or Greek motifs used in Samaria before Alexander, and papyri. There were boxes of small fragments and several well-preserved rolls. The writing was not Aramaic but Palaeo-Hebrew, written in Samaria, the earliest between 375 and 365 B.C. Many of the pieces had to do with real estate transactions, settlement of broken contracts, divorce and law agreements. There were also some pre-Alexandrine coins.

There was no doubt that these were the rebellious Samaritan leaders who had done away with Andromachus. They fled down the Wadi Farah into the wilderness to Wadi Dalyeh cave. There were whole families well supplied with food. Someone had betrayed them and the Macedonians had slain all of them.

The papyri are now being studied. It will be interesting to see what they reveal.

Alexander took over the whole of the Persian Empire, extending its borders to the Indus and Jaxartes rivers. Now Greek civilization touched the entire literate world. In the Far East the Greeks met China's borders in Turkestan; Chinese silk, fruit trees such as the apricot and citron came into western Asia and thence to Europe, while improved stocks of horses, asses, and swine were introduced into China. From India, which the Greeks had penetrated as far as the Ganges, came cotton, barnyard fowl, rice, the buffalo, asceticism, the monastic life, certain mystic points of view; position of numerals with zero; chess. Greek drapings and folds were given to the sculptured garments of Buddha; Greek architecture, astronomy, drama, and coinage became incorporated in Hindu civilization.

Throughout the new Greek province of practically all of southwestern Asia, including Egypt and North Africa, a single language, Greek, most often a Greek dialect, was spoken, so that people understood each other and ideas circulated freely. A unity of currency, new roads, improved harbors, lighthouses, and larger ships increased trade and contacts between peoples.

Alexander died in 321. His empire was divided among his

generals. At first Egypt ruled Palestine. The first Ptolemy carried off many Jews to Egypt as slaves. Ptolemy II liberated the Jews and allowed them to have their own quarter in the northeastern part of Alexandria near the royal palace. This grew into one of the largest and most influential colonies of Jews in the dispersion. There were colonies of Jews all over the civilized world, not only in Rome, Athens, Rhodes, Antioch, Damascus, Babylon, and Alexandria but in far off Spain and the upper reaches of the Danube. During the time of Ezra, the Torah or Law of Moses had been taken out of the hands of the priests and given to the people. Devoted teachers or rabbis taught the Torah to children in elementary schools, to youths in higher schools, to adults in the hall of study. The Jews became a people apart, because of their peculiar mode of living, their dress and religious views. The heathens could not understand why Jews would not eat with them, intermarry with them, or why they abstained from eating swine's flesh and warm food on the Sabbath. As a consequence the Jews were regarded as strange, enigmatic, mysterious people, who inspired awe, or they were treated with derision and contempt. The superficial pleasure-loving pagans regarded Jews as gloomy people who abhorred all the good things of life.

There were thoughtful discerning people who admired the Jews for their pure and spiritual worship of one God, their virtues of chastity, temperance and fortitude, and the bond of sympathy and affection which held them together. Thoughtful pagans were weary of immoral idolatry. Diogenes, the Cynic, dressed like a beggar, called himself "A Citizen of the World," and carried a lamp looking for an honest man. He preached that happiness is found in a simple, natural life. Zeno, the Stoic, shunned luxury, economic or political strife. To achieve peace of mind, he willfully obstructed all feelings and passions. The other extreme of this philosophy were the Epicureans, who held that the pursuit of pleasure was man's only true goal. Many Jews became Epicureans, especially the young and the rich. Stripped of clothing, they exercised in gymnasiums, superficially devoted themselves to science, philosophy, art, literature, the beauty and pleasure of song and dance, courtesans, drinking and feasting. These renegade Jews were fiercely opposed by the pietists or Hasidim who gloried in saintliness and kept the Mosaic Law to the letter. This has been described as the clash between Hellenism and Judaism, which resulted in the Maccabean revolt in 165 B.C. From the historical view the Greeks and Jews learned much from each other during this period, and their intellectual contributions became the basis for our western civilization.

Greek civilization opened doors to a different way of thinking which Jews entered eagerly and encountered true Greek philosophy which sought to explain the world through reason. The Greeks invented "Logic" which examined nature critically but with love for order, harmony, unity, and proportion, and beauty, so well exemplified in their art. The Hellenistic period was one of great creativity for the Jews, especially in the field of literature. Hellenistic Jews wrote in Hebrew, Aramaic, and Greek. In Greek literature Jews found exposures of the injustices and tragedies of life. The great masterpiece, the *Book of Job*, has for its theme the sufferings of the righteous, and was written around 400 B.C. About 200 B.C. a proverb writer, Ecclesiastes, or the Preacher, criticized the seekers after pleasure—"This also is vanity" he said, "and a striving after wind." Instead he counseled reverence and obedience to God. About 180 B.C. Joshua, Son of Sirach, whose book is called *Ecceliasticus*, wrote proverbs in brief poetic form extolling wisdom. In 130 B.C. his grandson, who bore the same name, translated this work into Greek. *The Wisdom of Solomon* was written in Greek about the first century B.C. This writer belonged to the Hasidim and taught that the moral life can only be attained through wisdom and the hope for immortality. His views were afterwards adopted by New Testament writers. According to George A. Barton, he was the first to identify the serpent of the garden of Eden (Genesis 3) with Satan (The Wisdom of Solomon 2:23, 24) and to account for the fall of man. Paul used this view in Romans 5:12-19. He also used the Word of God, as it is used in the Gospel of John.

The works of Judaeus Philo of Alexandria are an example of Hellenism influencing Judaism. He grounded his teaching on the Pentateuch and by means of allegorical interpretation read into it the philosophy of Plato and the Stoics. Philo influenced Christian theologians in later centuries.

Angels and Demons came into the literature during this period. In the Book of Daniel angels are given names like Michael and

Gabriel. The Apocalyptic writers of *Enoch, Esdras, Sibylline Oracles, Book of Jubilees,* and *Baruch* were obscure men who had a message and wrote in the name of some hero who had lived long ago and was revered in history. Their purpose was to give consolation and courage to those who suffered and were oppressed, and they used names of men like Jacob, Baruch, and Noah because prophecy was considered ended when the Great Assembly of Synagogue met in the third century. The prophetic works stood collected and were expounded alongside the Torah. These later-day prophets who wished to be heard wrote in the apocalypse style which became an accepted literary form between A.D. 200 and 100.

Some of the writers of this literature lived in Judea, others were residents of the great seaport Alexandria, business and intellectual center of the world. The Ptolemies who developed Egypt into a very prosperous country established a famous museum and library.

From the Marisa Tombs in southern Judah, archaeological remains bring to light a painted frieze. The models for the animals were taken by the artist from some book illustrating wild life in the famous zoological gardens in Alexandria.

Ptolemy IV ordered that every book brought to Alexandria should be deposited with the library. Copies should be made, the owner retaining the copy, the library the original. The office of librarian was one of the highest in the country, and one of the obligations of this office was to tutor the crown prince. A huge corps of copyists, many of them slaves, made duplicates of the precious originals, and scores of scholars separated the material into groups and established methods of textual and literary criticism. Many dictionaries and grammars were compiled by Hellenistic scholars to keep the ancient Greek language pure. Greek was spoken and understood all over the Near East and Egypt, but an oriental "pidgin Greek" had developed, and was even written in the cursive Greek script that made writing easy. There was a large reading public for writers who were producing hundreds of thousands of books. Many of them were written on papyrus, but the translation of the Hebrew Bible into Greek that was sent to the library in Alexandria was written on treated skins, of calves or sheep, called parchment.

The younger generation of the large Jewish population in Alexandria spoke Greek instead of Aramaic, the language of Palestine. To make the Word of God accessible to the Greek-speaking community, the Hebrew Bible was translated into the Greek language. Legend tells us there were seventy-two translators or seventy for short, which in Greek is Septuagint. This was the first attempt of the Jews to enlighten the Greek-speaking world about the Jewish conception of God and morality.

The King at Alexandria was very anxious to have the Hebrew Bible in his library. The Bible was written on leather. How the Septuagint translation looked was described in a letter of a certain Aristeas who lived in Alexandria in the third century B.C.:

"When they entered with gifts which had been sent with them, and the valuable skins on which the law was inscribed in gold in Jewish characters, for the skin was wonderfully prepared, and the connection between the sheets had been so affected as to be invisible, the king as soon as he saw them began to ask about the books. And when they had taken the rolls out of their coverings and unfolded the pages, the king stood for a long time; and then making obeisance about seven times, he said, 'I thank you my friends, and I thank him that sent you still more, and most of all God, whose oracles these are.' "

These scrolls were all of animal hide and written on the hairy side of the leather, which was specially treated. In later centuries the Talmud required all copies of the law to be written on skins in roll form. Even today, the "Torah" used in synagogues are written on parchment scrolls. Other Talmudic rules required that writers of scrolls rule the page horizontally with faint parallel lines with a hard stylus. The letters touched the top line in contrast to our writing where the bottom of the letter touches the lower line. The pages were separated from each other by vertical lines. Each writing sheet consisted of several pages, sewn together with dried tendons of flax threads. There were margins at the top and bottom of pages and between pages themselves. There was no punctuation, but an empty space of one or two lines indicated the end and beginning of chapters. The calligraphy of the writers was often a work of art. If a writer made an error by omitting a word or letter, he inserted it above the line at a suitable place. Dots above and below a script indicated it was superfluous and a mistake. A writer erased when the letter he needed was similar in form to one to be erased. He erased only part of it, and rewrote it in the form of the letter he wanted. If he started a wrong word, he left a space, and wrote the correct word. In later centuries these corrections produced discussion and controversy among scholars, who never realized the scribe had simply made a correction.

In Alexandria an international science developed pooling the natural philosophy of classical Greece with Babylonian and Egyptian disciplines. The Hellenistic scientists had Greek names and culture, but came from a cosmopolitan society.

Euclid (323-285 B.C.) produced his *Elements of Geometry*. Archimedes (282-242 B.C.) laid the foundation of mathematical mechanics. He invented the water screw and a pump or water-raising machine for irrigation.

Aristarchus (around 200 B.C. in cooperation with Babylonian scientists) developed the heliocentric theory that the earth and planets revolve around the sun.

Eratosthenes, director of the Alexandria museum, by using only sun dials and water clocks, figured out parallel and vertical lines around the earth called latitudes and longitudes. Ptolemy constructed a skeleton map of the globe on a frame of astronomically fixed latitudes and longitudes which have been in use since that time.

These are some of the mechanical inventions of the Hellenistic period. Few of them were used except in warfare. The great invention of this period was the rotary corn mill which consisted of two stones rubbing against each other, and pulled in a circular motion by an ass or slave. After 100 B.C. these mills were sometimes driven by water power. Glass blowing was developed to make retorts which were used in the development of alchemy and distilling alcohol. The use of lime mortar led to the Roman discovery of an almost indestructible cement by mixing lime with volcanic ash.

The inevitable question arises. Why weren't these inventions put to use? Why was pure science dead until the sixteenth and seventeenth centuries of our era? Hellenistic society had no use for mechanical servants when there were thousands of slaves to do the work.

Merchants and craftsmen profited from Hellenistic prosperity. Peasants became tenant or share farmers, and were often worse off than slaves. Delos was the international slavery mart, where human cattle were redistributed to Seleucia, Antioch, Alexandria, Carthage, Rome, Athens. The victims came from Britain, Russia, Spain, Morocco, Ethiopia, Iran, Judea, Armenia, Arabia. Some of these slaves were highly educated doctors, scientists, artists and craftsmen, who became court favorites, amassed wealth, and even owned slaves. Other slaves were criminals, laborers, prostitutes, or just an unfortunate human being. There were laws by which slaves could be freed and earn money. Often impoverished peasants joined with slaves in revolts. These were all brutally put down by armies.

Judea was an agricultural country, and life was hard for the farmers and workmen. Most of them were Zealots who found consolation in religion. Jerusalem prospered in Hellenistic times. The second Temple became the central shrine for the large colonies of Jews dispersed all over the world. Throngs of pilgrims came to see the pomp and ceremony, the music and singing of the Levites, the hundreds of priests, the gorgeous vestments of the high priest as he blessed the prostrate people in profound silence. Jerusalem was jammed with worshippers on the festivals of Passover, Weeks (the giving of the law), Tabernacles, and the awe-inspiring services of the New Year and Day of Atonement.

The wealthy classes who took Greek names, and hankered after pleasure, thus far received no opposition from the oppressed lower classes who bore their fate with piety and humility. In 165 B.C. when Antiochus Epiphanes outlawed the Jewish religion and was supported by renegade Hellenistic Jews, the Pietists supported the family of Maccabees, and won independence for their country. Under Simon Maccabeus, the Hasmonean dynasty was founded. There is ample archaeological evidence of Maccabean times at Beth-zur which commands the north south road from Jerusalem. This was excavated in 1931 by O. R. Sellers and W. F. Albright. Three hundred coins were discovered; some of them bear the names of Antiochus Epiphanes (171-164 B.C.) and his son Antiochus Eupator (164-162 B.C.). The second fortress is attributed to Judas Maccabeus (165-163 B.C.). At Beth-zur many wine jar handles from Rhodes and other Aegean centers give evi-

Courtesy Israel Department of Antiquities

Stamped jar handle of Maccabean period.

dence of a Greek garrison there in the Maccabean age. Approximately 2,000 jar handles were discovered at Samaria, another Hellenistic garrison.

Ruins of a fortress of Simon Maccabeus were found at Gezer. Simon reigned from 142-135 B.C. and the Jewish religion was faithfully observed, apostasy suppressed, material prosperity increased, and the courts were just. A grateful people designated him prince, commander, and high priest. His life was cut short when his son-in-law murdered him. He was succeeded by his son John Hyrcanus who ruled from 135-104 B.C. When he died the boundaries of Judea had reached the extent of Solomon's kingdom. Hyrcanus captured the fortress of the Idumaeans, Adora and Marisa, formerly Edomite country. Excavations revealed Marisa to be a typical second-century Hellenistic town with streets running at right angles forming regular blocks, and typical Greek houses, market place, and public buildings. Hyrcanus forced the Idumaeans to adopt Judaism as their religion. The independence of Judea was assured, and for the second time reached its highest peak of prosperity. He struck coins and inscribed them in old Hebrew characters with the words, "Jochanan, High Priest and head of the Commonwealth of Judeans." The Pietists objected to Hyrcanus controlling both the temple and state, for he had made peace with the aristocracy who had been in power under the oppressor Antiochus Epiphanes. When they found themselves in the minority in the Council of State, they withdrew from participation in the government and became the opposition. They became known as Separatists or Pharisees. Those priests who remained in the government were known as Sadducees. The differences went deeper than politics. The Pharisees had a different set of beliefs from the Sadducees who were conservatives and adhered closely to the Written Word of the Scriptures.

The Pharisees supplemented the Written Word by the oral traditions of the fathers they had learned by word of mouth, from Ezra who had adjusted the Mosaic law to the life of the times. The Bible was a living book for the Pharisees, and they adopted the beliefs and hopes of their generation; the Resurrection of the body and of judgment of the soul after death; they believed that God ordered the lives of men, but taught that men had freedom of will in their actions and were accountable for them. They recognized there were angels and demons, because in this world there is both good and evil; in the future the world will be all good, and evil will vanish like smoke, and God alone will reign. A messiah will bring about this era, and even now the pious Jew must so order his life as to be worthy of the Heavenly Kingdom which God will bring about in his own time. The Jew must pray that it will come soon. The religion of the Pharisees brought comfort to the lowly and was beloved by the common people.

Another extremely pious sect of Pharisees were the Essenes. They lived in villages located in the desert to the west of the Dead Sea, and settled in the Oasis of Engedi, where they tilled the soil, cultivated the date palm groves, worked at some craft but shunned commerce. After a double novitiate, they became full members. Children were admitted to be trained in the ways of the Order. They were all celibates, owned no personal property, for all property belonged to the Order. They bathed often and wore white garments, as did the priests in the temple who also wore white garments and bathed before officiating. The Essenes were called "Morning Baptists" because they bathed every morning in fresh spring water. Part of their ritual was eating their meals together and strictly observing the Sabbath. They sent offerings to the temple but no animal sacrifices. Rejecting all manner of oaths they cultivated prophetic clairvoyancy and practiced healing according to their studies of the medicinal properties of roots and herbs. They believed in the immortality of the soul and the will of God and that the Messiah would come in their day. From the Essenes it was said the prophecy was heard, "The Messiah is coming! The Kingdom of Heaven is near."

To the people this meant the Messiah would destroy their oppressors and restore the golden era of King David's kingdom. The Essenes were not only regarded as holy men because of their mode of life but also because of their miraculous cures of so-called "possessed persons." Their cures consisted of softly-spoken incantations and verses and the use of certain roots and stones which were supposed to have the power to cast out demons.

This briefly was the state of Jewish religious knowledge toward the end of the first century B.C. according to written records up to the year 1947. Then an Arab shepherd lad discovered the Dead Sea scrolls!

Our story begins in November of 1947 when Dr. Elazar L. Sukenik, professor of Archaeology at Hebrew University in Jerusalem, first glimpsed a scrap of ancient leather with some Hebrew writing through the holes of a barbed wire barrier.

Courtesy Hebrew University

Dead Sea scroll before it was unrolled.

"Is this old? Is this genuine?" asked his friend, an Armenian antiquities dealer, from the other side of the barbed wire.

Dr. Sukenik strained his eyes to make out the letter on the parchment and came to a quick decision. British soldiers were everywhere because of the tension between Jews and Arabs, who were awaiting the decision of the United Nations at Lake Success to create the State of Israel. It seemed to him the letters resembled the writing on small coffins and ossuaries he had discovered in tombs dating back to the period before the Romans destroyed Jerusalem. He needed to see more samples of the writing.

The Armenian dealer arranged to take him to Bethlehem to the Arab antiquities dealer, Feidi Salahi, who had Hebrew parchment scrolls, which he claimed were found in a cave near Jericho on the shores of the Dead Sea. The decision on Israel's independence had not yet been made the day Dr. Sukenik went to the attic of the Arab house where Feidi Salahi lived. He was the only Jew on the bus going to Bethlehem, and the Arabs' glances were hostile. Over coffee and the customary polite exchange of small talk, the Arab dealer told him how he came into possession of the scrolls.

Some Bedouins had been moving their goats along the northwestern shore of the Dead Sea. A fifteen-year-old boy, Muhammad Adh Dhib, "Mohammad the Wolf," searching for a stray goat, had stumbled across an opening in the rocks overlooking the sea. He threw a stone into the cave and heard a strange sound, as if the stone had broken a piece of pottery. He reported this to the other Bedouins, and the next day they crawled into the cave. They found themselves in a narrow crevice. On the floor were pottery jars, five on one side, three on the other. Several of the jars were covered with saucers. Inside the jars were bundles of leather, some of which were wrapped in linen. While reaching for the scrolls, they accidentally broke some of the jars. For weeks they wandered around with the scrolls, showing them to other Bedouins who came to their tent. Then they decided to go to Bethlehem, the commercial center of the Judean desert, and try to sell their find.

The Arab dealer brought out two of the jars that had contained the scrolls for Dr. Sukenik to inspect. Their shapes were un-

Courtesy Hebrew University

Pottery jars that contained the scrolls.

familiar to him. Then he showed Sukenik the scrolls. He unwrapped them and read a few sentences, which sounded like the Psalms, yet the text was unfamiliar. With pounding heart he looked at the beautiful Hebrew writing, and knew he was looking at a scroll that had not been read for more than 2,000 years.

Dr. Sukenik bought those scrolls for the State of Israel which within days came into being. Later, more scrolls were purchased from the Syrian Orthodox Monastery of St. Mark in Jerusalem. The scrolls were part of a huge library belonging to a Jewish Monastery. The texts were:

1. The Book of Isaiah, a leather scroll about 24 feet long with 54 columns of text.

2. A commentary on the Book of Habakkuk.

3. A Manual of Discipline: a book of rules governing the Jewish sect to which the library belonged, thought to be the Essenes.

4. Genesis Apocryphon, written in Aramaic.

5. Part of a scroll of the Book of Isaiah.

6. The War of the Sons of Light with Sons of Darkness, which was more than nine feet long when unrolled.

7. A collection of Thanksgiving Psalms.

Parts of over 100 scrolls of Old Testament books have been found. Every book of the Old Testament but Esther has been discovered. From studies made of the script, the earliest manuscripts are fragments of a scroll of Samuel and Jeremiah. Three different copies of the Book of Daniel were found, also the Book of Ecclesiastes. Most of the fragments showed little variance from the Hebrew text. Some texts are very similar to the Septuagint, which shows that the Greek translation does rest on a real Hebrew text tradition. The general date of the scrolls is either the first century B.C. or the early part of the first century A.D.

Père Roland de Vaux and G. Lankester Harding excavated Qumran for five seasons, and this is its archaeological history. In the seventh and eighth centuries B.C. in Israelite times it was a small settlement called City of Salt. It was abandoned for four centuries until the reign of John Hyrcanus (135-104 B.C.) when it was rebuilt by the Qumran community. Further development took the place in the reign of Alexander Jannaeus (103-76 B.C.) until a severe earthquake of 31 B.C. cracked cisterns and walls,

Courtesy Hebrew University

Cave at Qumran where the Dead Sea scrolls were discovered.

starting a fire which reduced the buildings to ruins. From 4 B.C. to A.D. 6 the community was restored until the Roman Legion violently destroyed the settlement in A.D. 68. At the end of the first century it was briefly occupied during the Second Jewish Revolt of Bar-Kochbah.

Excavation revealed how such a settlement existed in the desert. They caught and stored rain water, which rushed down the steep hills in the rainy season, in an elaborate system of plastered cisterns and canals. Purified in a large settling basin, the water was stored in seven large cisterns located near the work areas. Two baths were supplied with water, for bathing was a ritual with the group.

De Vaux judged the largest room of seventy-two feet by fourteen feet, nine inches to be their meeting room, and where they held their ceremonial meals, for in an adjoining room he found 1,080 pottery dishes consisting of 210 plates, 708 bowls, and 75 goblets. At the end of the long room was a circular paved surface which might have been the place where the president sat.

There was a complete pottery shop with a basin for washing

clay, a place for the potter's wheel, two kilns with furnaces located so they could catch the prevailing winds for drafts.

The scriptorium where they copied manuscripts might have been on an upper story from which had fallen fragments of a brick-like table about sixteen feet long and twenty inches high, as well as parts of several smaller tables. That these were copy desks was possible by the discovery of two ink-holders, one bronze, the other clay. In one of them was some dried ink.

The Manual of Discipline states the principles of their faith which are rules of behavior in accordance with the laws of God, given "through Moses and through all his Servants the prophets; to love all that He has chosen and to hate all that He has rejected; to keep away from all evil and to adhere to all good deeds; to do truth and righteousness and justice in the land . . ." All those who are accepted as members are "Sons of light," and pledge themselves to "Love all Sons of Light . . . and to hate all Sons of Darkness each according to his guilt in the vengeance of God."

This sect was influenced by the religion of Zoroaster, in the

Courtesy Hebrew University

Parchment as it came out of the scroll.

conflict of good and evil, light and darkness. G. Ernest Wright parallels this with the New Testament in John (12:35): "He who walks in the darkness does not know where he goes. While you have the light believe in the light that you may become sons of light."

Some scholars of the past tried to relate John to Greek philosophies, but have encountered difficulties. The discoveries of Qumran provide a background for John's thinking as well as that of Paul (Ephesians 2:2), who describes the struggle against the powers of darkness who are agents of "the prince of the power of the air, the spirit that is now at work in the sons of disobedience."

The Dead Sea scrolls present some new facts connected with the foundation of Christianity and the influence of Judaism. G. Ernest Wright is of the opinion, "The study of this question is only beginning and will occupy the attention of scholars for many years to come."

According to Frank Moore Cross, Jr., "The most direct and obvious contribution of the Qumran scrolls is in the field of Old Testament studies."

Before the discovery of the Dead Sea scrolls, the earliest known Masoretic, or traditional Hebrew text, of the Hebrew Bible dated back to A.D. 895, a papyrus book in the Synagogue of the Karaites in Cairo, Egypt. The Septuagint or Greek translation of the entire Old Testament is Codex Vaticanus in the Vatican Library dating from about A.D. 350.

About A.D. 100 the authoritative Hebrew text was fixed—the time of Rabbi Akiba. The question was: From what Hebrew text was the Greek Bible translated, in the third century B.C.?

Many Apocryphal documents were found in Cave IV, written both in Hebrew and Aramaic, among them Tobit, Jubilees, Enoch, the Book of Daniel. The Isaiah scrolls found at Qumran were about 500 years older than the earliest Greek version of the Septuagint. They belong to a period when there was no standard text, and yet are almost identical with the Masoretic text standardized in A.D. 100. There are two Isaiah scrolls in Israel at the Hebrew University. There are many minor differences between them. These scrolls, according to Yadin, prove the antiquity and authenticity of the Masoretic text.

The scrolls also revealed that the Septuagint was a faithful translation of historical books like Samuel, Joshua, and Kings. The text of Jeremiah, which in the Septuagint is one-eighth shorter than in the Hebrew Bible, must have been translated from a shorter text similar to one found at Qumran. Dr. Frank Moore Cross, Jr. writes, "The new finds will chart new courses by which progress will be made toward a more accurate, more intelligible Old Testament."

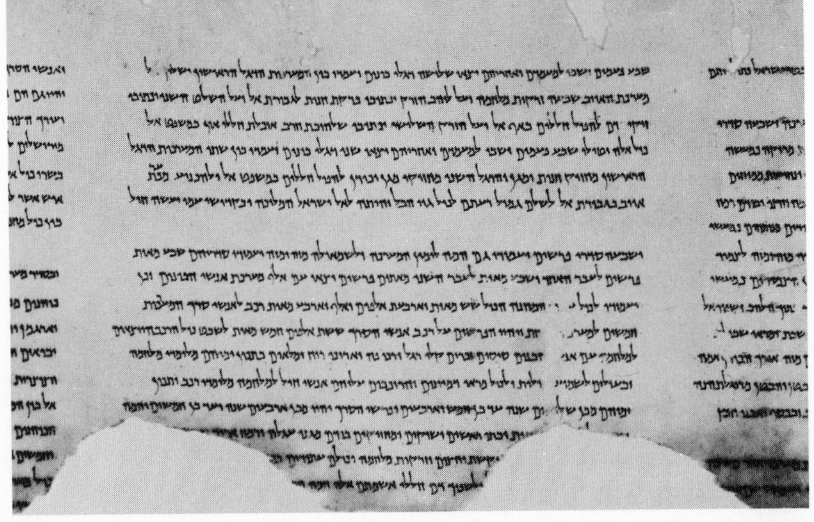

Courtesy Hebrew University

Parchment after it had been cleaned and mounted.

CHAPTER XIX

ARCHAEOLOGY AND CHRISTIANITY

THE OLDEST MANUSCRIPTS of the New Testament were found in the Egyptian desert. Papyri were found buried in the sand. The dry Egyptain climate had preserved a fragile papyri fragment of the Gospel according to John, 18:31: "Then said Pilate unto them, Take ye him, and judge him according to your law. The Jews therefore said unto him, it is not lawful for us to put any man to death."

According to the handwriting, the papyrus is dated in the first half of the second century A.D. 125. This earliest of manuscripts was discovered in 1935 among some papyri in the John Rylands Library in Manchester, England, that B. P. Grenfell had acquired in Egypt in 1920. It was written in a well-executed literary script, the precursor of what is known as "Uncial." This is derived from the Latin word "uncia," meaning the twelfth part. So an uncial character took one-twelfth of a line. This large, beautiful script was easily read and was used for literary and sacred writings. It took a great deal of time.

In Roman and Byzantine times, the ordinary script used for business and letters was not dignified enough for writing the Bible and literary works. A beautiful handwriting, which we call calligraphy, was developed, but was known as Minuscule script. The writer wrote continuously without raising the pen, which speeded up his work. By the ninth century A.D. all the manuscripts were written in minuscule script. This was used as long as books were copied by hand.

In the first century manuscripts were written without punctuation or spacing between words, and the quotation from John (18:31) would look like this:

THENSAIDPILATEUNTOTHEM
TAKEYEHIMANDJUDGEHIMACCORDINGTOYOUR
LAW.

Ammonius of Alexandria and Eusebius of Caesarea divided the Gospels into sections. These are known as the Ammonean Sections and Eusebian Canons. The system of chapter divisions for the New Testament was done by Cardinal Hugo de S. Caro in 1238. Robert Etienne, known as Stephannus, introduced modern verses in 1551.

The pens were usually made of reeds which had been dried, sharpened to a point, and split into two parts. Ink was made of lamp-black, gum, and water. The ink was very black and did not fade.

These manuscripts came in rolls, or in book form, which were called Codex. The material was either parchment or papyrus. We discussed the use of leather for writing in connection with the Dead Sea scrolls. Most of the New Testament manuscripts were written on papyrus.

From earliest times the Egyptians made papyrus for writing material, and we derive our word "paper" from it. Paper, as we know it, made from rags, bark, and hemp fibers, was invented in China by Ts'ai Lun in A.D. 105. It was used in Egypt around A.D. 900 but not in England until 1494 after printing was introduced. Europeans used paper parchment before this.

Papyrus was made from the plant of the same name which grows in the Egyptian marshes. The papyrus stalks were split with a needle into very thin leaves. These were glued together with Nile water, which is like glue when it is muddy. The jagged edges were cut off and a cross layer placed on top of the first long sheet. The leaves were pressed together and dried in the sun. Then the sheets were taken off one by one and glued together to make a roll. There were never more than twenty sheets in a roll. These were exported all over the ancient world as writing material.

Christian writers favored the Codex which, like modern books, were bound in quires: a sheet of papyrus folded in the middle, thus forming two leaves of a folio of equal size.

The part of the New Testament attributed to Paul was originally letters written on sheets of papyrus. These were collected, copied, and bound into a codex or book form.

In 1778, an unknown antiquities dealer from Europe was in Egypt during a cold spell. He noticed some Egyptians feeding a fire with rolls of papyrus, which gave off an aromatic odor they enjoyed. They had already burned up about fifty rolls of manuscripts, but the dealer managed to buy a roll and bring it back to Europe. Since that time the Egyptian desert has been a veritable storehouse of ancient papyri. The Fellahin, or peasants, like the Bedouin of Palestine, are constantly on the lookout for papyrus rolls, because they know they can sell them to antiquity dealers.

In the nineteenth century, Flinders Petrie found a quantity of manuscripts while excavating an Egyptian cemetery. Papyrus manuscripts were used to line mummy cases. At a place called Gurob, where crocodiles were worshipped and mummified, archaeologists found the crocodiles wrapped in papyrus manuscripts, and some of them were stuffed into the animals' mouths or cavities in their bodies.

A century ago the oldest manuscripts of the New Testament were *Codex Vaticanus*, a vellum parchment text written about A.D. 350, and another old parchment, *Codex Sinaiticus* of about the same date. The *Codex Vaticanus* has been in the Vatican Library at Rome as early as 1475. The *Codex Sinaiticus* was found in the Monastery of Saint Catherine in Sinai by a German scholar, Constantine Tischendorf, in 1859. He had won a reputation as a critic and decipherer of ancient manuscripts. The Tzar of Russia subsidized his trip to Palestine for research and discovery. While first visiting the library of the monastery in 1846, he noticed a large basket filled with old parchments. The librarian told him these were destined for the flames since they had become mouldy. Tishendorf looked through the supposed refuse and found a copy of the Old Testament in Greek written in the most ancient script he had ever seen. The authorities allowed him to take about forty-three sheets from the basket. In 1846 his patron was the King of Saxony, so he titled the parchment *Codex Friderico*

Augustanus. In 1859 when the Tzar was his patron he returned to the monastery and he was about to leave without finding anything. Then the steward of the monastery invited him to his cell. There he gave Tischendorf a bulky volume wrapped up in a red cloth. Tischendorf not only found the parchments he had seen in the basket fifteen years before, but other parts of the Old Testament, the New Testament complete, the Epistle of Barnabas, and a part of the Pastor Hermas. The Tzar paid the monks $6,750 for the manuscript. The *Codex Sinaiticus* remained in Leningrad until the British purchased it from the Soviet Union in 1933 for $500,000.

In 1936 and 1937 the Colt Archaeological Expedition worked at Nessana in the Negev in southern Israel. In Byzantine times this was a stopping place on the caravan route from Eilat to Gaza. Buried in the debris of a room annexed to a small church they found papyri of the New Testament, a copy of the apocryphal correspondence between Abgar and Christ, a version of the legend of St. George, and a portion of the Twelve Chapters on Faith. According to one of the papyri, this church took part in the business life of the city. The presbyter was also the chief money lender, and his interest charges were considerably higher than the legal rate. According to Jack Finegan the total number of Greek New Testament manuscripts is about 4,680, without Latin, Syrian, and Armenian.

It must be kept in mind that the oral traditions of the Gospel were in Aramaic, the language of Jesus. The Gospels were not written in Greek until the dispersion of the Jewish Christians before the first revolt in A.D. 70. They were treated as Jews by their pagan neighbors and persecuted as pacifists and defeatists. James, the brother of Jesus and head of the Christian community, had been killed before the revolt. The Christians fled to Pella before the revolt. The oral traditions and eyewitness accounts of the apostles had dimmed by the time the Gospels were written down in Greek in various parts of the Roman Empire.

Early Christian tradition regarded the Gospel of John as greatly influenced by the Greek world. Since the translation of the Dead Sea scrolls, particularly the scroll of the War of the Sons of Light against the Sons of Darkness, and the Manual of Discipline, John in some ways seems to be the most Jewish, instead of being the most literary and latest of the Gospels. Some scholars now think it the earliest, and its tradition was that of Jerusalem before the destruction in A.D. 70. The Gospel of St. John presented a more intimate view of Jesus. According to W. F. Albright, names like Mary, Martha, Elizabeth, Salome, Johanna and Sapphira are not anachronistic or out of place in the Gospel of John, because they were the common names of the period, like Jesus and Joseph. Ossuary inscriptions (receptacles of bones) found around Jerusalem in tombs dating to the last decades before the destruction of the Second Temple A.D. 70 are inscribed with the above names.

The Essenes were not early Christians. They followed the Jewish tradition of seeking salvation in the Mosaic Law or Torah, as preparation for the Messiah and his kingdom. Like the early Christians they thought the prophecies of the Old Testament prophets were coming true in the events of their own days. The Essenes wrote from Isaiah, "When these things come to pass in Israel to the Community . . . they will separate themselves from the midst of the abode of perverse men to go into the desert to prepare there the way of the Lord according as it is written, 'In the desert prepare ye the Way (of the Lord), make straight in the wilderness a highway for our God.' "

In Matthew 3:1-2 it is said, "In those days came John the Baptist preaching in the wilderness of Judea, and saying, 'Repent ye: for the kingdom of heaven is at hand.' "

"For this is he that was spoken by the prophet Isaiah saying: 'The voice of one crying in the wilderness. Prepare ye the way of the Lord, make his paths straight.' "

So the disciples of John the Baptist and those of Jesus followed the same principles as the Essenes, accepted a special discipline in preparation for the establishment of God's Kingdom on earth. Both communities had twelve leaders. Their central rites were baptism and the communal meal. Acts 2:42 says, "And they continued steadfastly in the apostles' doctrine and fellowship and in breaking of bread and in prayers."

There was no personal property. All property of the Essenes was held in common. According to Acts 4:32, "Neither of them said that aught of the things he possessed was his own; but they had all things in common."

Courtesy Israel Department of Antiquities

Ossuary—early type clay receptacle for bones.

The war between Light (Righteousness) and Dark (Evil), the idea of two forces fighting to make a good man, is very much like the Gospel of John as well as the language. In John 8:12 it is said, "I am the light of the world; he that followeth me shall not walk in darkness." The Essene text from the war is, "For they are of the portion of darkness, while the portion of God is everlasting light."

Frank Moore Cross, Jr. writes, "We should emphasize that the New Testament was not a new faith, but the fulfillment of an old faith. . . . The New Testament does not set aside or supplant the Old Testament. It affirms it and from its point of view completes it."

Archaeology was the science through which the late Professor E. L. Sukenik first recognized the antiquity and significance of the scrolls. Study of them by scholars has shed new light on Biblical texts and on the Hebrew and Aramaic languages. They are a literary product of a sect who sought to escape from the troubled times out of which Christianity was born. They show the influence of Zoroastrianism on Judaism at that time, in the War of Light and Darkness. They reveal parallels with the New Testament.

The Dead Sea scrolls are not Christian for they contain none of the theological doctrines of the Christian faith. They are a new source of information regarding New Testament times and thinking.

CHAPTER XX
ROME MOVES IN

IT WAS A SABBATH MORNING in the month of Sivan (June, 63 B.C.) that the Roman general Pompey took advantage of the Jewish strict observance of the Sabbath and conquered Jerusalem. The legions of Rome pushed into the courts of the Temple, killed the priests as they stood sacrificing before the altar. It is said 12,000 Judeans died that day, some by throwing themselves headlong from the battlements, while others were slaughtered by the Romans. When the Roman general entered the Holy of Holies and saw no images, he was reported to be so filled with awe that he did not touch the Judean treasury of 2,000 talents. He had just finished conquering and plundering western Asia and had amassed a vast fortune. Judea was made tributary to Rome.

Palestine, with the entire East, was affected by the civil war between Pompey and Julius Caesar in 49 B.C. Caesar was assassinated on the Ides of March 44 B.C. Mark Antony who formed an alliance with Octavian, a nephew of Caesar, defeated Cassius, one of the conspirators against Caesar, and became master of western Asia.

While the weak Hasmonean princes quarreled among themselves, and a band of Zealots in Galilee was attempting to stir up a revolt for the restoration of Jewish Independence, a young man from Idumaea called Herod seized the leader of the revolt and a number of his followers and had them executed. The Council of State, now called by the Greek name of Sanhedrin, summoned Herod to trial. Through the influence of his father

Antipater who was governor of Idumaea and advisor to Hyrcabus, the nominal ruler of Judea, Herod was acquitted. Thus began the career of this grasping ruthless upstart who became known as King of the Jews, when the Maccabean or Hasmonean dynasty ended in 37 B.C. This was accomplished by having Mark Antony appoint him a Tetrarch or co-ruler of Judea with Rome. With the help of two Roman legions, Herod captured Jerusalem, and Antony at his request beheaded the last Hasmonean ruler Antigonus. In the meantime Antony had become enamored of the Egyptian queen Cleopatra, and compelled Herod to cede to her rich districts about Jericho with palm and balsam forests. These Cleopatra leased out at a high rental. In 32 B.C., when Octavian declared war against Antony and Cleopatra, Herod double-crossed his former friends, supplied the Roman Octavian with provisions, and helped defeat Antony and Cleopatra. Herod got back the balsam and palm forests at Jericho, as well as the coastal cities of Jaffa and Gaza. He even murdered his wife Miriam whom he loved passionately, because of false accusations of his mother and sister. Herod was deeply grieved over Miriam's death, tried to forget her through wild dissipation, and became ill. When Miriam's mother attempted to restore the Hasmonean dynasty, Herod quickly recovered and executed the plotters.

Now at the height of his power, Herod cultivated the friendship of Octavian who had become Augustus Caesar, Emperor of Rome. Herod's power was absolute in a domain that once more extended to the limits of David's kingdom. With trade overseas from Mediterranean ports, and caravans from the Far East stopping at Jerusalem, the country was very prosperous. Barren land was put under cultivation and all of Judea intensively farmed. People were heavily taxed. Herod was very rich from revenues from his own estates, interest on loans to neighboring rulers, and from working the imperial copper mines in Cyprus. He spent money lavishly. Herod reigned until A.D. 4. Four years before he died of cancer, a child called Jesus of Nazareth was born in Bethlehem. This event went unnoticed by the great king for the boy was the son of a workingman. Herod, like Solomon, was a great builder and supposed his monuments would keep his name alive. The buildings of Herod have become ruins in the dust, while Jesus of Nazareth has become immortal.

Another immortal of Herod's reign was Hillel, who came from Babylon. He was a Pharisee, a liberal thinker, who is remembered for his patience, gentleness, and humility. In answer to a heathen who asked to be instructed in the Jewish religion in the shortest time possible, Hillel answered: "Do not unto others what is hateful to thyself; this is the whole of the Torah, all the rest is commentary."

Archaeology has excavated some of Herod's constructions. He built harbors, large waterworks, and aqueducts. In Jerusalem he repaired the city fortifications and rebuilt the second Temple. At the northwest corner of the Temple area he rebuilt a citadel and called it "The Tower of Antonia."

On the western hill he constructed for himself a magnificent palace, with huge halls of marble and decorated with gold and rare stones. The Temple, or original structure from the description of Josephus, was increased in height, and built of huge blocks of white stone. Only priests were employed in the building of the Holy of Holies, to which laymen were not admitted. A large porch ran across the front down which descended twelve broad steps to the Court of the Priests with the Altar and the great Laver. Next followed the Court of Israel for men worshippers. Separated by a wall was the gallery for women. Lower down, the Court of the Gentiles was divided from the Inner Sanctuary by a wall and fenced-off terrace. A Greek inscription forbade any foreigner to go in under pain of death.

Only Herod's masonry walls have been found by archaeologists. In 1894 and 1897 F. J. Bliss and A. C. Dickie found remnants of a wall which might have been the southern wall of Herod around the western hills, but these have not been dated. C. N. Johns excavated in the Citadel at the Jaffa Gate between 1934 and 1940. Beneath the courtyard of the Citadel was found a pre-Herodian wall of the third and second centuries B.C. curving southward and strengthened by three towers. The foundations of one of these ancient towers still support the present "Tower of David." The stones in this substructure weigh as much as five and ten tons; they are beautifully cut and jointing is very close. They may be a remnant of Herod's three towers.

Kathleen M. Kenyon excavated in Jerusalem in 1961-63. Her conclusion substantiated the findings that early Jerusalem lies to the south of the present old city. Perhaps this excavation will give further information about Jerusalem.

Crowfoot excavated Samaria, which became the Roman city of Sebaste. He found a temple which Herod had built for the worship of the emperor, and a stadium for athletic events. The standing masonry at Samaria is good but not as fine as that of Jerusalem. The podium on which the temple of Augustus stood and foundations of the stadium belong to the period A.D. 120-230.

Herod built Caesarea in honor of the Emperor Augustus by the sea on the site of an old Phoenician town called Strato's Tower, between Joppa and Dor. According to Josephus, "He adorned it with a haven that was always free from the waves of the sea." Herod erected a temple "that was seen a great way off by those that were sailing for that haven, and had in it two fine statues, the one of Rome, the other of Caesar." Herod also built a theater of stone; and on the south quarter behind the port, an amphitheater "capable of holding a vast number of men."

In 1960 archaeological excavations were made under the direction of Professor Antonio Frova. In the same year they cleared and unearthed the Roman theater. In 1960 an American industrialist and engineer, Edwin Link, used his own specially constructed vessel for underwater archaeological exploration, and investigated Herod's submerged harbor. In the same year the Israel Department of Landscaping and Preservation of Historic Sites, Prime Minister's Office, excavated, cleared, and landscaped the site. The entire site was cleared, roads were built around the city, ancient walls and churches were restored, and the area was posted with explanatory signs so that modern Caesarea is one of the finest tourist attractions in Israel. Monuments belonging to Roman, Byzantine, and Crusader periods have been uncovered.

Now we are concerned with the monuments from Herod's time. The Roman theater has now been restored, and there Israel annually holds an International Music Festival. The Roman hippodrome where Titus killed thousands of prisoners after the sack of Jerusalem in A.D. 70 in gladiatorial games has not yet been excavated, but it is possible to gain an idea of its size —1,056 feet long and 264 feet wide, holding 20,000 spectators. When the Italian expedition excavated the theater they unearthed a stone inscribed with the name of Pontius Pilate, Roman governor of Judea at the time of the Crucifixion. Until this time Pontius Pilate was only known from the New Testament and the writings of Josephus. Josephus described subterranean vaults that carried sewage off to sea. Excavators found remains of a sewage channel more than six feet deep.

The Crusader fortifications in the Middle Ages were constructed from the ruins of Roman buildings. Foundations of the temple and buildings Herod erected facing the harbor have been identified by pottery and finely crushed sandstone packings. One vaulted construction was intact and contained numerous Byzantine storage jars. This may have been originally a Roman warehouse and continued to be used as a warehouse by the Byzantines.

Herod's most spectacular building was his winter home at Masada on a cliff overlooking the Dead Sea. This fortress was erected shortly after he seized power. Josephus tells us the reason. "... Herod's fear of the multitude of Jews lest they should depose him and restore their former kings.... Cleopatra queen of Egypt ... spoke often to Antony and desired him to cut off Herod, and entreated him to bestow the kingdom of Judea upon her." Josephus described the rock of the fortress as so steep no animal could climb up, and surrounded by valleys so deep the eye could not see their bottoms. There were two entrances: one toward the Dead Sea on the east, and a winding trail on the west called the "Serpent." The first fortress on Masada had been built and named by Jonathan, the High Priest. Herod built a white stone wall around the hill with thirty-eight towers, each of them fifty cubits high. The king reserved a portion of the top for a garden because the soil was very fertile and would assure a food supply. At the western entrance he built a palace facing north. Four high towers at each corner of the palace served as lookouts. Josephus tells of a great variety of cloisters and baths, and the floors made out of many colored stones or mosaics. Out of the rocks he cut many reservoirs for water.

Archaeological excavations at Massada have shown Josephus to be a very accurate historian from his description of the palace. No wonder, for he was living during the time of the Jewish revolt against the Romans from A.D. 68-73, and witnessed the sack and destruction of Jerusalem. He writes, "I Joseph the son of

Matthias, by birth an Hebrew, a priest, also one who at first fought against the Romans myself, and was forced to be present at what was done afterwards."

This was during the period of the debauched Nero who committed suicide and left no successor to the throne of Rome. Vespasian, a tough general, seized power and sent his equally hardened son Titus to Judea to quell the rebellion. Josephus commanded a post in Galilee, where Rome was expected to strike first. He bungled his command and escaped with forty of his companions to a cave. He wanted to surrender to the Romans, but his companions insisted they all die together, each by the sword of his companion. The last man alive would commit suicide. Josephus was the last. Preferring life to death, he surrendered himself to the Romans and lived to become the historian of the Jews.

Recently Professor Yigael Yadin excavated Massada and found more Biblical scrolls. According to Père de Vaux these scrolls may have been the work of the Essenes at Qumran whose settlement by the Dead Sea was destroyed by the Romans in A.D. 68. Some of the Essenes may have taken refuge in Massada with the Zealots. This is merely conjecture. The scrolls found at Massada are similar to those of Qumran.

The Temple in Jerusalem was destroyed and the treasures carried off to Rome by Titus, where his arch of triumph still stands in the ruins of the ancient Forum in modern Rome. A bas-relief of a seven-branched candlestick of the Jews can still be seen on the arch of Titus in Rome. Jewish resistance continued from Masada, and they held out for two years. When the Romans at last entered the fortress, they were confronted by the stillness of death. The band of defenders—men, women, and children—had killed themselves.

CHAPTER XXI
ROME TAKES OVER

The steadfast love of the Lord never ceases, His mercies never come to an end.

(LAMENTATIONS 3:22)

THUS PRAYED the orthodox Jews of modern Jerusalem in Israel on the night of the ninth of Ab, which fell on a very chill night in early August. They swayed, they wept in the red glow of bonfires and candlelight. Loud speakers blared the voice of the leader who chanted the prayers, perhaps in the hope that the echo of his prayers would cross the no-man's land between Israel and Jordan to the remnant of the wailing wall of the second temple which still is standing in old Jerusalem in the Kingdom of Jordan.

Some of the tourists who crowded the hill to watch the ceremonies could not understand why these people still mourned and wept for a building that was destroyed in A.D. 70 and would never be rebuilt again.

They did not understand that reciting prayers from the Book of Lamentations gave hope and renewed faith to a people who had survived the Romans, the Torquemadas, the Czars of Russia, and Hitler.

The Wailing Wall was a symbol of a faith that had withstood the milleniums. Johannan, son of Zaccai, realized that the second temple had become a symbol, when he made the decision to leave Jerusalem while it was still being besieged by the Romans in A.D. 70.

Over a period of four years the Romans had been trying to conquer Jerusalem. There were famines and epidemics, and only the dead left the city, and that was for burial.

Johannan pleaded with the Zealots who defended the city: "Surrender, and save the city. Do you want to see the Temple go up in flames?

The Zealots were adamant. They would not surrender; neither would they allow any of the people to leave the city. Johannan determined to escape. He knew the second temple would be destroyed and he was helpless to save it. He could save Judaism and all it stood for—the Holy Scriptures—the Torah!

According to legend he conceived the idea of taking refuge in the camp of the Roman General Titus, who was passionately enamored of the beautiful Jewish princess Berenice. Perhaps because of his love for Berenice the Roman would not deny him asylum.

Among the Zealots Johannan had a friend Ben-Batiach who conveyed Johannan's message to Titus in a very novel way; he wrote it out on a piece of papyrus and shot it by arrow into the Roman camp. The message said that at sunset of that day Johannan Ben Zaccai would be carried out of Jerusalem in a coffin. Johannan desired peace and the permission to found a center of learning at Jabneh, or Jamnia.

Just as the sun went down, Johannan in a coffin was carried through the gates of Jerusalem by his pupils, Eleazar and Joshua. Titus himself received the fugitive and granted his request to settle in Jabneh and found a center of Jewish learning there. Whether Berenice had anything to do with this is not known. Neither had she the influence to prevent Titus, when he captured Jerusalem, from razing it to the ground, taking the people prisoners and killing the young men in gladitorial combats in the arena at Caesarea. The most handsome and vigorous men were picked out for the triumphal procession in Rome.

At Jabneh, Johannan Ben Zaccai built up a center of Jewish learning in the tradition of the Pharisees. He knew the day of the second temple had ended with its animal sacrifices. He envisioned a new destiny for Judaism—a spiritual destiny, and with this vision he made Jabneh the national religious center for the dispersed community. He organized a new Sanhedrin, which he called Beth-Din (Court of Justice). Johannan was the first president. He founded a school for the study of the law in the tradition of Hillel which allowed for the adjustment of the law to progress. Johannan ordained Gamaliel the second of the family of Hillel as his successor. All future presidents were appointed in this manner.

Gamaliel organized divine worship and gave it form. Now all worship was held in synagogues. On the Sabbath and holy days, sections of the Torah were read. The Rabbis translated the law into Aramaic so that the people could understand it, and explained the law through sermons. The scrolls, carefully wrapped in linen, were kept in a chest called the Ark. Other chests were used for the storage of the rest of the books of the Scripture. Any man in the congregation who conducted himself with dignity might pass before the Ark and lead in the services. A special desk was kept for Scripture reading. Attached to every synagogue was a Bible school for children and youths. The Hall of Study was the highest department of education, and was attended by scholars. It was the duty of the community to help poor and fatherless children receive an education.

There are no archaeological remains of first-century synagogues because the Romans destroyed all the synagogues after the first and second revolts. Between A.D. 66 and 70, over 480 synagogues in Jerusalem alone were destroyed according to Jewish tradition. The Essene community at Qumran was demolished during this period.

The second Jewish revolt broke out in A.D. 132. From caves, fortified towns, strongholds, the Jews waged guerrilla warfare. Rabbi Akiba led the revolt with Simon of Cozeba, whom he proclaimed as the Messiah and named Bar Kochbah, which means "star." Coins struck by the general had a figure of the temple surmounted by a star. The revolt was caused by the announcement of the Roman Emperor Hadrian that Jerusalem was to be converted into a pagan city, and the issuance of a law forbidding circumcision.

Jerusalem was captured, and an altar set up. Bar Kochbah's uncle ministered as priest. Only one Roman legion guarded the city. The first victory was easy, the rebels virtually walking in. They held Jerusalem for two years.

Rabbi Akiba, noted for his keen intellect and learning, had been, according to legend, an illiterate shepherd in his youth. He fell in love with a rich man's daughter and in order to win her followed her bidding that he acquire an education. The Song of Songs for Akiba symbolized the union between God and Israel and was his favorite book in the Scriptures. He is famous for arranging the Oral Law according to subject matter. This was given the name of Mishnah (Study).

Hadrian at last sent one of his best generals to Judea, and the rebels were defeated in A.D. 134. In chapter three the Roman City of Aelia Capitolina which displaced Jerusalem was described. All of Palestine was impoverished by the Roman wars.

In the meantime, Bar Kochbah and his followers held out at Beth-zur, southwest of Jerusalem. By A.D. 135 those that had not died of starvation were killed or enslaved by the Romans. Half a million Jews were said to have died. Those who were sold at Hebron fetched no more than a horse, there were so many Jewish slaves for sale. Rabbi Akiba was executed. Nothing was known about Bar Kochbah except his coins. In 1953 a cave was found on the shore of the Dead Sea at Ein-Gedi that contained Bar Kochbah's dispatch case as well as the remains of rebels who had escaped to the cave.

At the end of the year 1951 more scrolls began to appear on the antiquities market. Scholars observed from the script that they were of later origin than those of Qumran. Harding and de Vaux, the excavators of Qumran, negotiated with the Bedouins who had found scrolls to buy them and find out where they came from. Père de Vaux asked the Bedouin leader how much he wanted for the scrolls. The Bedouin opened a cigarette box and showed de Vaux some fragments of scrolls. The price he asked was unreasonable.

De Vaux would not even consider buying them.

Then the Bedouin said it was hard work finding these pieces of old scrolls. The caves were so huge, it took forty or fifty Bedouin workers days and weeks to find these few pieces in the box.

De Vaux shook his head dubiously. What was so difficult picking up these few pieces of parchment?

"If you don't believe me come and see," said the Bedouin.

"What about the police?" asked de Vaux.

"We have guards all over the hills," said the Bedouin. "If the police appear, our guards flash signals, and our men disappear into the caves and behind rocks.

Then de Vaux suggested that if the Director of Antiquities of the State of Jordan accompanied them, the Bedouins would have nothing to fear from the police.

In January, Harding and de Vaux, an Arab foreman, a police escort and the Bedouin guides reached the new caves about twelve miles southwest of the Qumran caves and east of Bethlehem. They were in a gorge between cliffs 600 feet high. Three miles ahead was the Dead Sea. The caves were in the cliffs that faced north, 200 feet above the floor of the gorge. De Vaux was now sure he had come to the right place, because Bedouin diggers darted out of the caves to hiding places. He counted thirty-four of them. They found four caves and more scrolls. The excavators were sure these caves were the source of the flood of documents appearing on the market. These caves had not only been used in Roman times, but thousands of years earlier: the Chalcolithic Age, the Early Bronze Age; the Age of the Patriarchs and the Kings of Judah in the eighth and ninth centuries; their remains were found in tools, pottery, scraps of papyrus and scrolls from later periods than the Qumran texts, mostly Biblical books. They found a complete phylactery with the Hebrew prayer, the Shema. "Hear O Israel, the Lord our God, the Lord is one."

Greek and Hebrew documents, mostly dated letters and contracts, show that Bar Kochbah was the name given the leader of the revolt by Rabbi Akiba. A letter in which he wrote to one of his commanders, Yeshua Ben Galgola, is signed Simon Ben Kosebah, Prince of Israel.

Bar Kochbah's letters show him to demand absolute discipline, and he punished all who disobeyed him.

In 1954 the Department of Antiquities in Israel sent expeditions to investigate caves in Israel. In the deep Hever Valley they found the caves had been ransacked by Jordan Bedouin. Roman camps were found on top of a mountain overlooking a deep canyon. In a cave 85 meters below the top and 50 meters above the valley floor, the excavators entered by means of a rope ladder. They found a number of skeletons, men, women, and children, people who did not surrender to the Romans during the Bar Kochbah revolt.

In 1961 Yigael Yadin of the Hebrew University explored Nahal Hever near Ein Gedi on the west bank of the Dead Sea. Besides volunteer workers, members of Israel's defense army took part. The canyon was 1,300 feet high and an army helicopter flew in and spotted and photographed the caves.

Men were lowered 300 feet down the cliff on ropes. Because of the danger of avalanches it was a very risky business. The caves were bat-infested, and the men had to crawl on their stomachs through rocky corridors to reach the inner cave. There they found a collection of baskets containing human skulls and layers of mats covering human bones. These were the remains of Bar Kochbah's fighters.

The army had a walkie-talkie down in the river bed below. One of the soldiers got stuck in a crevice of a rock and yelled, "Basket full of skulls!" They got him out of the crevice and the explorers with candles and torches crawled to the back room 450 feet inside the rock. The ceiling was covered with soot, showing the cave had been occupied after an avalanche of rocks had fallen from above.

They found rugs woven with thirty-three different colors, parts of tunics. These were similar to the Roman tunics—a panel in front, a panel in back, a slit for the head.

By using a mine detector they found it reacted violently about 50 feet from the entrance. They dug into the floor of the cave and found a basket on its side, both handles tied together with a rope. This contained some copper jugs engraved with heads of birds and palm motifs. Some incense shovels, and a pan engraved with a ram's head. Names of Roman gods had been scratched out. Evidently this was part of Bar Kochbah's booty from the Romans. They found a coin with the stamp, "For the freedom of Jerusalem," a triangular-shaped Roman arrowhead, wool and linen yarn that had never been used, a bone spoon, a salt stone, a peppercorn, and a collection of papyri. These were wrapped in a ripped goatskin bottle.

The collection of papyri was separated by strips of wood. These were orders from Shimon Bar Kochbar Hannasi al Yisrael, Simon bar Kochbar, Prince of Israel.

One letter concerned the confiscating of the wheat of one Tahnun Bar Yishmael, who was to be sent to Bar Kochbah under guard. Another letter signed by Schmrel Ben Ami, an adjutant of Bar Kochbah, warned the people of Tekoa in the desert of Judea, that unless they cooperated with Bar Kochbah they would be punished.

The unfolding of the papyri was a most meticulous procedure. There were fifteen documents: four in Hebrew; nine in Aramaic; two in Greek letters were from Bar Kochbah. These letters show us how he dealt with the people and gave orders. Evidently not all the people sympathized with his cause. About another 150 meters inside the cave another waterskin bag was found. When opened, it spilled out the pathetic evidence of the transient quality of human possessions. This was a woman's bag with sandals similar to those worn by women today. There were two keys on a ring, a mirror, some brass flasks, a knife with a wooden handle, a beautiful glass set, and a huge net, 10 yards by 10 yards. Bamboo sticks protected some papyrus documents. One letter written in colloquial Hebrew said in relation to the feast of Tabernacles, "I'm sending two donkeys and two men ahead with palm branches, citron and willow for the celebration of Succoth."

Evidently this woman had a wealthy father, for there was a deed written in Nabataean script regarding a grove her father had bought from some Nabataeans. When this woman escaped into the cave she evidently took along correspondence to use as evidence in a lawsuit. She was being sued by the relatives of her two deceased husbands.

For 2,000 years the desert preserved this woman's possessions, which at that time meant so much to her, and today merely give us a glimpse into the life of that day. This was the last futile attempt of the Jews to gain independence. There were uprisings in Byzantine times but they were quickly put down by the Romans.

Rabbi Akiba died a martyr's death along with ten other scholars. Hadrian kept the country under military rule; the observance of the Sabbath, teaching of the Torah, and maintaining a religious organization was forbidden to the Jews. Hadrian died in A.D. 139 and his successor, Antonius Pius, was the most loved of Roman rulers. During his reign Roman peace and prosperity reached its zenith. The empire reached the frontiers of all the known civilized world by conquest. The army was corrupted by the discovery that is was more profitable to plunder the civilized world than to defend it against barbarians.

The Romans were great builders; their arched bridges and aqueducts still stand. But they destroyed more of civilization than they built. Rome did not try to assimilate the conquered subjects. They were free to follow in the way of their fathers, as long as they obeyed the authorities, kept the peace, and paid taxes. The excessive burden of taxes was the chief cause of the downfall of the West. The loss of an industrial market was caused by provinces like Britain, the south of France, and Germany, who were making their own pottery and weaving cloth. Roman craftsmen migrated to the provinces and set up industries to escape excessive taxation and competition from slave labor. Syrians had migrated to the Rhine valley and established a glass-making industry. Transportation over the good roads and in the small ships was slow. The home market had fewer and fewer buyers. The luxuries imported from the Far East, like dancing girls, parrots, ebony, ivory, pearls, precious stones, spices, and perfumes from India, and silks and drugs from China, were paid for in gold. By A.D. 250 Rome was drained by the Orient of her stocks of gold and silver and was practically bankrupt.

The capitalistic farms had become huge estates, whose owners were exempt from taxation. Freeholders and urban workers took refuge on these estates to escape the tax gatherers. These estates began to resemble the feudal estates of the Middle Ages, with their own potteries and every kind of craftsmen—weavers, fullers, smiths, carpenters. First Tiberius denied slaves the right to strike. Then Diocletian, in the fourth century A.D., froze people into their hereditary occupations. This applied especially to tenant farmers, who were not free to leave the land to which they were attached by birth. If they tried to leave they would be brought back in chains and punished. The tenant farmers had become serfs in the days of Constantine, the first Christian emperor.

Free shows and free grain could not revive industry and trade and stave off economic collapse. There was no progress in technology. Romans still used the ancient halter on draft animals, which strangled their windpipe and impeded their speed pulling freight along the roads. No Roman ever thought of a harness, nor of improving the clumsy rigging of their ships. They made no contributions to pure science, philosophy, or religion. They produced lawyers, administrators, teachers of rhetoric. Their system of education neglected the natural sciences and practical subjects.

The Romans were literary. During the first century B.C. almost every city in the Mediterranean area had a public library. The great Greek libraries were located at Rhodes, Athens, and Alexandria. Augustus built and enlarged libraries in Rome. Herod in Jerusalem built a library whose books are listed in the works of Nicolaus of Damascus. The discovery of the Dead Sea scrolls has acquainted us with the library of the Essenes. The first century A.D. was a time of learning and scholarship. The Romans did not succeed in guarding ancient learning against the Dark Ages.

It was said of Hillel, who lived at the time of Herod, and Yohanan Ben Zaccai, of Roman times, that they knew all the teachings of the wise men including languages and sciences. Ben Zion Wacholder writes in *Nicolaus of Damascus*: "The evidence assembled indicates that there existed no iron curtain between Judaism and Hellenism, at least not in the second half of the first century B.C. Hillel was not averse to blending Greek ideas with Pharasaic Judaism." Jewish scholars must have been familiar with Greek and Roman learning. The makers of the Mishnah from A.D. 135 to 175 were compilers and gatherers of the Oral Law into one book. This type of literary work was typical of the Roman scholars who wrote many histories and compendiums, or compilations.

After the Bar Kochbah revolt and defeat, the Rabbis moved the Sanhedrin to Galilee, with centers of learning at Tiberius, Sepphoris and Beth-shearim.

It is remarkable how these scholars managed to survive so many catastrophies, and yet they kept on with their mission of producing literary works, and keeping the Jewish community together. Their strength lay in their religious belief, and the messianic hope of the Kingdom of God. The basic Jewish teaching of giving charity brought help from Jewish communities outside of Palestine, particularly in Babylonia where millions of Jews lived in Roman times.

Judaism was a teaching of the law, the Torah. It had to be

Courtesy Hebrew University

Beth She'arim, entrance into catacombs at bottom of hill.

learned and taught so that the people would understand the prayer, "Hear O Israel the Lord thy God is One." For this reason learning was regarded as a virtue among the Jews. The two great works, the Mishna and the Talmud were written between the first century B.C. and A.D. 400. The city of Talmudic learning was Beth She'arim.

For centuries, southeast of the modern Mediterranean port of Haifa between the Carmel range and the lower Galilee highlands, there was a gentle, sloping mound, surrounded by cultivated fields. In 1936 the accidental discovery of a tomb cave caused Professor Benjamin Mazar, a past president of the Hebrew University, to excavate the site. World War II interrupted the work, and it was resumed by Professor N. Avigad from 1953 to 1957. The mound turned out to be a tremendous underground cemetery. The dead were buried in underground rooms, connected by halls and galleries or catacombs. Jewish catacombs from the first century have been found in Rome and are marked with Jewish symbols like the menorah or seven-branched candlestick, and the Star of David. The early Christians also buried in catacombs. W. F. Albright writes regarding their similarity to Jewish tombs: "The third-fourth century necropolis at Beth She'arim in Palestine has already demonstrated the previously unsuspected extent of early Christian dependence on Jewish art of the Roman period."

The first excavations revealed the main buildings of the city on the northeastern part of the mound and the catacombs lying on a semi-circle north and west of the city area. One of the buildings in the city was a large synagogue, probably the largest in Galilee. It is in the formal basilica style with a main hall containing a nave and two side aisles separated by two rows of columns. Marble slabs covered the plastered wall, ornamented with carvings and inscriptions. There are remains of several public buildings, dwelling houses, a glass factory, an olive press, and a hoard of coins. No coin bears a later date than A.D. 350. Most are from the period of Constantine the Great and Constantinius II. One of the public buildings of the usual basilica type oriented east-west may have been the study hall of the sages. A large installation for extracting olive oil was found down the slope on the northern edge of the tell connected with a dwelling house of the sixth and seventh century A.D. This shows that the town was rebuilt after the Gallus revolt in 351 when the Romans destroyed the city, and continued until the Arab conquest.

The cemetery is cut deep into the rock, a palatial underground city of the dead, with vaulted halls, and rooms richly ornamented in bas-relief, fresco and grafitti, depicting human busts, animals, birds, facades of houses, geometric designs. There were inscriptions in Hebrew, Aramaic and Greek, showing that many Jews living in Syria and Phoenicia brought their dead here for burial. Each catacomb had its own entrance closed by stone doors, which are still in good condition, made of a single stone slab sculptured and decorated with geometric designs to look like paneled wood. One of the most monumental of tombs may possibly be attributed to the family of Rabbi Yehuda Hannasi, the compiler of the Mishna.

Some of the most interesting synagogues are those from the first half of the fourth century when Rabbi Abbun gave official permission to have mosaics representing living creatures used in decoration. The most beautiful is the mosaic floor of the sixth-century Beit Alpha Synagogue at Beit-Shean. The synagogue at Capernaum, third century A.D., is a basilica type with elaborately carved stone ornaments in the form of shells, grapes, eagles, and palm trees. To the east was a colonnaded court, part of which still stands.

Not all synagogue building was confined to Galilee. Near Nirim in the western Negev Mr. S. Levy excavated a synagogue with an Aramaic inscription in a mosaic pavement at the northern end of the central nave, which commemorates the whole community for contributing money for the mosaic floor, and especially mentioning three people who gave money for the Scroll of the Law. The mosaic floor is very well done in different designs and colors, and looks very similar to a floor of a Byzantine church excavated in 1917 which dated A.D. 561. The same artist may have laid both floors.

During the ten years from 1948 to 1958 the Department of Antiquities reports that eight ancient synagogues previously unknown were found, five of which were explored. Most of them are from the fifth and sixth centuries, with mosaic floors. The beautiful colors and rich variety of designs of mosaics in both synagogues and Christian churches reveal a period of religious art unknown before archaeological excavation.

The Nabataeans

The mosaic of Palestine would not be complete without a glimpse at the Nabataean civilization. In 1812 a Swiss traveler, Johan Ludwig Burckhardt, discovered the ancient Nabataean city of Perta in ancient Edom, south of the Dead Sea. in Transjordan. Cut from cliffs with as many changing colors as the Grand Canyon were houses, temples and tombs. Even free standing pillars in front of temples and tombs were carved out of the rock, as were the stone staircases leading up to them. Petra became a spectacular site for nineteenth-century tourists, and remains one of the most picturesque sites of modern Palestine. Petra was excavated under the direction of George Horsfield in 1929, who found three stages of pre-Byzantine occupation.

1. From the fourth century B.C. to the first century B.C.
2. From the first century B.C. to the Roman occupation A.D. 106.
3. A submerged period under the Romans.
4. The Byzantine period.

Edward Robinson back in 1839 discovered a number of high places where the Nabataeans worshipped. In 1934 W. F. Albright excavated a high place on the highest section of the walled city and found among other things a processional path around a sacred rock. In 1937 Nelson Glueck excavated a Nabataean temple on top a high hill called Jebel et-Tannur southeast of the Dead Sea. This was set on a platform with a large courtyard in front. The Nabataeans worshipped Hadad, identified with the Greek Zeus. Next to him was the female goddess Atargatis, who was like the Greek Artemis, a personification of fertility powers.

Petra is entered by a winding passage two kilometers in length and not more than ten meters wide. This is called the Siq. The sandstone cliffs are lined with tombs and chapels of a cult of the dead. Early tombs are Mesopotamian and Egyptian in decoration. Tombs of the second period are Hellenistic.

Aretas was the Nabataean king at the height of their power, 9 B.C. to A.D. 40. His kingdom included southern Palestine, the Negev, most of Transjordan, northern Arabia, and—at the end of his life—Damascus. This was the King of Damascus who tried to seize Paul. He escaped through a window in a wall by being let down in a basket. Herod Antipas, the son of Herod the Great, married a daughter of Aretas. Herod Antipas deserted her for his sister-in-law, Herodias, whom he married. John the Baptist told him it was unlawful to marry his brother's wife, and Herod put John in prison. According to legend Herod celebrated his birthday with a feast, and Salome, the daughter of Herodias, danced for the king. He was so enthralled, he said he would give her whatever she asked. At her mother's prodding she asked for the head of John the Baptist. So John was beheaded and his head was given to Salome on a platter, which she presented to her mother. Herod's first wife, the daughter of Aretas, fled to her father, who sent an army against Herod Antipas and defeated him in A.D. 36. In those days Petra was one of the merchandise marts of the East, with caravans from India and China stopping on their way to either Syria in the north or Egypt in the south.

Nelson Glueck, who made a survey of Transjordan and the Negev, discovered over 500 Nabataean villages, cities, and fortresses. The Nabataeans conquered the desert by trapping water in cisterns, building dams, and terracing the hills with stepped-

Courtesy Israel Department of Antiquities

Thamudic inscriptions found along the old caravan roads in the Negev.

back rows of large, roughly-hewn limestone blocks, which are still intact after 2,000 years. They literally turned a desert into a garden, and produced enough food to feed the populations of many villages and cities that grew up in the desert.

Nelson Glueck located the many Nabataean sites by picking up fragments of very thin pieces of pottery. These belonged to beautifully shaped plates, bowls, cups, and various kinds of jugs. Designs of leaf and floral patterns were painted in reddish brown on a buff background. Bands of rouletting were used as decoration. Coins, bits of glass and potsherds were found at a Nabataean caravanserai that was still standing at the end of World War I when the stones were used to build a police station. The Nabataeans were a trading people and worked the copper mines in Sinai. Along the caravan routes Glueck found rock drawings of helmeted warriors on camels or on foot with drawn swords. There are Thamudic and Arabic inscriptions, and petroglyphs of hands, feet, games, and tribal signs.

After the Roman conquest the Nabataeans declined. Roman roads by-passed Petra. Palmyra, situated in an oasis in the central desert of Syria, boomed as a trade center.

With the advent of Christianity and the rise of Constantinople, the trade routes through the Negev were revived. The Nabataeans were converted to Christianity, and in the reign of Justinian were incorporated into a district of their own called Palestina Tertia. In the sixth century A.D. the Negev prospered once more. The Nabataean methods and techniques of water and soil conservation were continued by the new generation of Christians, who now called themselves Byzantine, and the Nabataean people disappeared as a distinctive people with a unique culture. They discontinued writing in their own script, and no longer manufac-

Three apses of church at Shivta.

tured their beautiful pottery. But their cities of Avdat and Shivta still stand.

Shivta was also discovered by Edward Robinson in 1839. It was excavated in 1935 under the direction of Harris D. Colt. In Shivta you see the remains of a Byzantine town. The streets are narrow, but some of the stone houses, even with a second story, still stand. Narrow windows keep out the blistering desert sun. There are built-in pottery pipes which channel the water from the flat roofs to cisterns below the living quarters. In the main square are well preserved cisterns, and the remains of a fine church with a columned nave. Shivta had a population of about 6,500 people in Byzantine times. Beyond the eastern side of the square is a wine press, with a paved platform on which the grapes were crushed, the juice flowing through a channel to a round vat cut in the floor of a lower room. There are three churches in Shivta, but the north church is the latest and largest, with three apses. It was paved with marble and the walls partly faced with marble. Adjoining it is a chapel with a mosaic floor of geometric design. Five hundred meters away to the north are the remains of the fields and irrigation system of a Byzantine farm.

With the Moslem conquest in 643 came the decline of cities in the entire region and the end of Nabataean culture.

During the Byzantine period churches and monasteries covered every holy place mentioned in the Bible. The sands of centuries covered many of the Byzantine ruins until they were discovered after World War II by Israeli archaeologists. During the period from 1948 to 1956, twenty-nine ancient churches, chapels, monasteries and monastic farms were discovered in the modern state of Israel, which extended from the north to the south of the country. Most of them were paved with richly colored mosaic floors, with designs of birds, animals and plants. There were inscriptions in Greek and Syriac. A large church with many mosaics gave the dates of construction and repairs in the fifth century A.D. In the Negev, the most interesting Byzantine monuments are those churches built in the towns of the Nabataeans who had been converted to Christianity.

So ends our dig into the ancient lands of the Bible. The greatest treasure we found was the learning. The Bible becomes more precious and valuable not only as a source of spiritual inspiration, but as a living record of the history and learning of the ancient world. It is impossible to dig into the past without realizing that the learning of mankind must never be lost again. We must guard the learning of both the past and the present, and pass it on to our children, so that never again a Dark Age will blacken the face of the earth.

Base of preaching platform of church at Shivta.

BIBLIOGRAPHY

Albright, William Foxwell. *Archaeology of Palestine.* London: Penguin, 1963 ed.

———. *From the Stone Age to Christianity.* Anchor Books, 1957.

Aharoni, Yohanan, and Amiran, Ruth. "Arad, A Biblical City in Southern Palestine," *Archaeology,* Vol. 17 (Spring 1964), 49-53.

Amiran, Ruth. *Ancient Pottery of Erez-Yisra'el.* Israel: Ministry of Education and Cultural Department of Antiquities, 1958.

Atiqot. *Journal of the Israel Department of Antiquities.* Jerusalem: Ministry of Education and Culture, 1959.

Barton, George A. *Archaeology and the Bible.* 7th ed. Philadelphia: American Sunday School Union, 1949.

———. *The Religion of Ancient Israel.* Perpetua Edition. New York: A. S. Barnes & Co., Inc., 1961.

Bewer, Julius A. *The Literature of the Old Testament.* New York: Columbia University, 1933.

Breasted, J. H. *Development of Religion and Thought in Ancient Egypt.* New York: Harper Torchbook, 1959.

Brockelmann, Carl. *History of the Islamic Peoples.* New York: Capricorn Books, 1960.

Budge, E. A. Wallis. *The Rosetta Stone.* The Trustees of the British Museum, 1951.

Cassuto, U. "Baal and Mot in the Ugaritic Text," *Israel Exploration Journal,* Vol. 12, No. 2, 1962.

Cipolla, Carlo. *The Economic History of World Population.* Baltimore: Penguin Books, 1962.

Chiera, Edward. *They Wrote on Clay.* University of Chicago Press: Phoenix Books, 1938.

Childe, Gordon V. *Man Makes Himself.* Mentor Books, New American Library, 1955 ed.

———. *What Happened in History.* Baltimore: Pelican Books, 1964 ed.

Clark, Grahame. *World Prehistoric Outline.* Cambridge University Press, 1961.

Cross, Frank Moore Jr. Epigraphic notes on Hebrew Documents of the 8th-6th Centuries B.C. American Schools of Oriental Research, Jerusalem Baghdad No. 165 (February 1962), 34-36.

———. *The Ancient Library of Qumran.* Garden City, New York: Doubleday & Co., Anchor Books, 1961.

———. "The Discovery of the Samaria Papyri," *The Biblical Archeologist,* Vol. XXVI, No. 4 (December 1963).

Dhorme, E. "La Question des Habiri," *Revue de l'histoire de Religions,* No. 118 (1938), 153-158.

Dudley, Donald R. *The Civilization of Rome.* New York: The New American Library, A Mentor Book, 1960.

Durant, Will. *The Life of Greece.* New York: Simon & Schuster, 1939.
Erman, Adolf. *The Literature of the Ancient Egyptians.* London: Methien & Co., Ltd.
Finegan, Jack. *Light From the Ancient Past.* Princeton University Press, 1959.
Gaster, Theodor H. *The Dead Sea Scriptures.* Anchor Books, 1964.
Gelb, I. J. *A Study of Writing.* Chicago: University of Chicago Press, Phoenix Books, 1963, 2nd ed.
Glueck, Nelson. *Rivers in the Desert.* New York: Farrar Strauss and Cudahy, 1959.
———. *The Other Side of the Jordan.* American Schools of Oriental Research, 1940.
Graelz, Heinrich. *History of the Jews.* Philadelphia: Jewish Publication Society of America, 1940, Vol. II.
Greenberg, Moshe. *The Hap/piru.* New Haven: American Oriental Society, American Oriental Series No. 39, 1955.
Grousset, Rene. *The Civilizations of the East.* New York: Alfred Knopf, 1929.
Gurney, O. R. *The Hittites.* Baltimore: Penguin Books, 1964 ed.
Harden, David. *The Phoenicians.* London: Thomas and Hudson, 1962.
Helbeck, Hans. *Plant Economy in Ancient Lachish.* Oxford University Press, 1958.
Herskovits, Melville J. *Man and His Works.* New York: Alfred A. Knopf, 1950.
Holt, John Marshall. *The Patriarchs of Israel.* Vanderbilt University Press, 1964.
Holy Scriptures. Philadelphia: Jewish Publication Society of America:
Josephus, Flavius. *History of the Jews.* William Whiston translation.
Layard, Henry, Sir. *Early Adventures in Persia, Susiana and Babylonia.* New York: Longmans Green, 1887.
Kenyon, Kathleen M. *Archaeology in the Holy Land.* New York: Frederick Praeger, 1960.
———. *Beginning in Archaeology.* New York: Frederick Praeger, 1962 ed.
———. "Excavations in Jerusalem, 1961-63," *Biblical Archaeologist,* American Schools of Oriental Research Jerusalem and Bagdad, Vol. XXVI, No. 4.
Kroeber, A. L. *Anthropology.* New York: Harcourt Brace & Co., 1948 ed.
Margolis, Max, and Alexander, Marx. *History of the Jewish People.* Philadelphia: Jewish Publication Society, 1927.
Mazor, Benjamin, and Schweig, S. J. "Perfume Factory of King Josiah," *London Illustrated News* (April 16, 1964) 546.
McCowne, D., and Keith, Sir Arthur F. R. S. *The Stone Age of Mount Carmel,* Vol. 11, Oxford Clarendon Press, 1939.

Mendenhall, George F. "Mari," *Biblical Archaeologist*, Vol. XI, No. 1, (February, 1948), 2-19.
Meyerhoff, Hans. *The Philosophy of History in Our Time. An Anthology*. New York: Doubleday Anchor, 1959.
Muller, Herbert J. *The Loom of History*. New York: Mentor Book, American Library, 1961.
Nathan, H. "The Skeletal Material from Naval Hever. Cave No. 8," *Atigot*, Vol. III, Jerusalem.
The Oxford Annotated Bible; Revised Standard Version of the Holy Bible. New York: Oxford University Press, 1962.
Petrie, Turville. *The Stone Age of Mount Carmel*. Oxford Clarendon Press, 1939.
Pritchard, James B. *Archaeology of the Old Testament*. Princeton University Press, 1958.
———. *The Ancient Near East. An Anthology of Texts and Pictures*. Princeton University Press, 1958.
———. *Gibeon*. Princeton University Press, 1962.
———. *The Ancient Near East in Pictures Relating to the Old Testament*. Princeton University Press, 1954.
Rawlinson, George. *A Memoir of Major General Sir Henry Rawlinson*. New York & Bombay: Longman Green & Co., 1898.
The Readers Bible, Authorized Version. New York: Oxford University Press, 1951.
Roth, Leon. *Judaism, A Portrait*. New York: Viking Press, 1961.
Rowley, H. H. *From Moses to Qumran*. London: Lutterworth Press.
Sandars, N. K. *The Epic of Gilgamesh*. Penguin Books.
Schevill, Ferdinand. *The History of the Balkan Peninsula*. New York: Harcourt Brace & Co., 1922.
Smith, Robert Houston. "The Household Lamp of Palestine in Old Testament Times," *Biblical Archaeologist*, Vol. XXVIII, No. L, 1964.
Speiser, E. A. "Ethnic Movement in the Near East in the Second Millennium B.C.," *Annual of the American Schools of Oriental Research*, IXIII, 1933, pp. 13-54.
Schaeffer, Claude F. *The Cuneiform Texts of Ugarit*. Oxford University Press, 1939.
Thompson, David. *England in the Nineteenth Century*. Pelican Book, 1963.
Vaux, Roland de. *Ancient Israel: Its Life and Institutions*. London: McGraw Hill, 1961.
Wacholder, Ben Zion. *Nicolaus of Damascus*. University of California Press, 1962.
Wilson, John A. "The Apiru of the Egyptian Inscriptions," *American Journal of Semitic Languages & Literatures*, XLIX (1933), 275-280.

———. *The Culture of Ancient Egypt*. University of Chicago Press: Phoenix Books, 1963, 9th ed.
Woolley, Leonard, Sir. Abraham: *Recent Discoveries and Hebrew Origins*. New York: Scribners, 1936.
———. *Digging Up the Past*. Penguin Books, 1961 ed.
———. *A Forgotten Kingdom*. Penguin Books, 1953.
Wright, G. Ernest. *Biblical Archaeology*. Philadelphia: The Westminster Press, 1957.
Yadin, Yigael. *The Message of the Scrolls*. New York: Simon & Schuster, 1957.
———. *Hazor*. Jerusalem: Magnes Press, 1958.
Yeivin, S. H. *A Decade of Archaeology in Israel, 1948-58*. Netherlands, 1960.

INDEX

INDEX OF BIBLICAL CITATIONS